"Rock 'n' Roll will be gone by June."
Variety magazine, early 1955

The **first** shoes were found painted on Spanish caves dating back to 13,000BC; the first boots did not appear until 1000AD. Roman soldiers found that as they marched **north** into **Europe** their open Mediterranean sandals were too exposed and they were thus forced to adopt an enclosed **shoe**.

Designed by Phil Gambrill, Martin Roach and Kaye Roach.
Concept, production and project management by Gary Pettet,
Martin Roach and Independent Music Press Ltd.
Text by Martin Roach.

Printed in Italy.

Introduction

Hippies didn't wear Dr. Martens. They wore baseball boots or, in my case, a pair of corduroy lace-ups that caused such damage to my feet and such pain that when I remember to do so, I still walk with a slight but interesting limp. Well, I remember reading as a boy that Virgos often limp and I'm a Virgo. Not that I really believe in that sort of thing of course. But throughout the Seventies and Eighties I kinda yearned for a pair of Dr. Martens, only making my move when I realised that I was the only member of the family who wasn't wearing a pair. I bought a conventional pair of black 12-holers in Ipswich. My wife, Sheila, came with me. She knows that I like shopping about as much as I like flying; ie. not at all. She currently owns five pairs of Dr. Martens: two cherry reds, one with steel toe-caps, one without, a light green and a dark green and a purple. This morning she's wearing the dark greens.

I'm still wearing the black ones I bought in Ipswich six or seven years ago. I wear them almost every day. Some of the stitching is awry and there is a centimetre long cut on the right boot where my toe-nail has slashed its way through the leather. A little water comes in when it's wet but not much. There's a drawing pin stuck in the bottom of the left boot also and there is, I'm afraid, dried dog shit down there as well. These things will pass though, the dog shit sooner than the drawing pin.

I also have a green pair of Dr. Martens, more laces, but they're still covered with mud from the last Glastonbury festival and lead a quiet and lonely life outside the kitchen door. They're a size too big anyway because Sheila wasn't with me when I bought them. So, I panicked and said, "I'll take those. No, they're fine," paid and made my escape.

When I die, the children will probably argue over who gets my boots. "They're so typical of Dad," one of them will say fondly. "Especially the dog shit," another will add and they'll all laugh. Kids, eh?

John Peel

the Genesis of an Icon

The decade in which the Dr. Martens boot was born saw an unprecedented wave of change, new ideas, cultural upheaval and eventually social revolution. Along with this radical atmosphere came extravagant and often exotic fashions, which provided a rather incongruous backdrop for the infancy of such a functional boot. The contraceptive pill was launched in the same year as the Dr. Martens boot, and this single-handedly revolutionised many women's lives - within seven years, the 'Summer of Love' and the intoxicating redolence of all things psychedelic was everywhere, but for now the plain, simple Dr. Martens boot was as far from fashion as it seemed possible to be.

So how did it make that change? How did it transform from a workwear boot that was at one point sold as a gardening shoe, into one of the definitive subcultural icons of the twentieth century? It is a strange story...

The bizarre tale begins in the pedestrian town of Wollaston, Northamptonshire, in the English Midlands. The year is 1901. Benjamin Griggs and Septimus Jones decide to form a boot-making partnership, drawing on the county's history of making fine, hand-crafted footwear. After Jones left the partnership in 1911, Benjamin recruited his son Reginald and mother Jane - it has been a family business ever since.

Thereafter, the Griggs family settled down to earning a solid reputation for hard-wearing, solidly built workwear - mainly heavy screwed and stitched miners and army boots. In light of the latter-day association with

Dr. Maertens

Bill Griggs

skinheads, it is interesting to note that one of their best-selling models at this early stage was the Bulldog boot. These were bought en masse by the army and marched their way through two World Wars.

The story now switches to post-War Munich, 1945, and Dr. Klaus Maertens, a 25 year old soldier fighting at the Front. During a spell of leave from combat, he broke his foot after a bad ski-ing fall in the Bavarian Alps. Whilst convalescing, he thought of a possible remedy for his injury - a sole made of some type of air-filled material rather than the conventional harder leather. Dr. Maertens later said "The week war ended, everyone rushed out and started looting. But while most people were looking for valuable stuff like jewels and furs, I picked out a cobbler's last, some leather, needles and threads and made myself a pair of shoes with the thick air-cushioned soles I'd been thinking about."

With his rather crudely hand-made prototype boots on his feet, Maertens made his way south to Munich to generate interest in his invention. By chance Maertens bumped into an old University friend, Dr. Herbert Funck. He was born in Luxembourg but raised in Germany, and the two had met at Munich University - indeed, for a while they both vied for the affections of the same girl.

Funck was fascinated with the peculiar shoes on his friend's feet. After talking for a while, Funck - a mechanical engineer - suggested they go into partnership together making the sole. He had kept hold of his Luxembourg passport, so the current ban on trading with the American military did not apply - he quickly bought up tonnes of rubber from abandoned Luftwaffe airfields at rock bottom prices and began converting them into shoe soles.

Speaking in 1985, Maertens reflected on their fortunes: "Our timing was perfect. The whole of Europe had just spent five years in army boots and everyone knew how uncomfortable they were. The shoe was the right answer at the right time." The two friends used various bits of old army uniforms to construct these early shoes: "I pulled the regimental numbers off my jacket epaulets and used them as eyelets, and I bought uniform trousers from ex-officers for their leather leggings. I could get two pairs of shoes out of one pair of trousers. But the secret was all in the soles..."

In 1947, the two men started hand-made shoe production in the town of Seeshaupt. The early versions were a cross between a brothel creeper and a boot. The new footwear proved exceptionally popular, especially with old women, such that by 1952 they were forced to open a factory in Munich. Throughout the '50s, 80% of their shoes were sold to women over the age of 40, in a variety of over 200 different styles. By 1959 they had decided to advertise their invention in overseas trade magazines.

Dr. Maertens and Dr. Funck

"I'm **happy** that **new life**'s been injected into **the boot**..."

Dr. Klaus Maertens.

Back in Britain, the teenager had arrived. The new Labour government had ushered in an era of relative prosperity following the grim days of the war-time ration book. With it had come the first teenage phenomenon - the Teddy Boy. Dressed in Edwardian clothes, pointed boots and later brothel creeper shoes, the Teds marked the beginning of modern youth subculture.

For the Griggs Company, however, this blossoming of youth culture did not generate any extra sales, despite Prime Minister Harold Macmillan's famous words that "people have never had it so good." By the '50s, competition was getting tougher, in particular from the so-called Tuf boot. The company was now run by Bill, the third generation of the family, along with brothers Ray and Colin, and son Max. They were all anxious to scout for new products, and whilst scanning the pages of the trade magazine, *Shoe & Leather News*, Bill's eye was caught by the German Doctors' aforementioned advert. He immediately got in touch.

So it was that Griggs acquired the exclusive licence to produce the air-cushioned sole. A few key changes were made before it was launched - the elongated German heel was altered to a more rotund and orthodox shape. As the intention was to market the boot as workwear, a strong leather upper with a distinctive bulbous shape was attached, with a distinctive yellow welt stitch. Griggs further developed the famous look of the footwear and designed a two toned grooved sole edge and unique sole pattern. The new name for this brand made by Griggs with the air cushioned sole was AirWair. The brand was further signalled by a black and yellow heel loop featuring this word and the slogan "With bouncing Soles." This script was based on Bill Griggs' own handwriting and was taken directly from the doodles he drew when coming up with the brand name.

An early advert for DM's

Also in 1959:
Rock's first
martyrs,
Richie Valens,
Buddy Holly and
Big Bopper all
die in a plane
crash in Iowa;
Barbie Doll
launched;
Panty hose
invented.

Also on April 1st:
1928 HMV release the
first automatically
changing record
player for £128;
1969 John Lennon is
quoted in *The Daily
Express* as saying
"I'm down to my
last £50,000";
1984 Marvin Gaye
is shot dead by
his father.

1.4.

Legend has it that the original boot was intended to have an oily finish, suitable for use in the fish markets of east London. However, a rogue batch slipped through uncoated and proved to be equally durable and more appealing to the eye.

Finally, the name was anglicised. Hence, on 1st April, 1960, the very first Dr. Martens boot rolled off the production line. Taking its name from the date of its inception, the eight hole, cherry red 1460 had arrived.

60

Music in 1960:
'Itsy Bitsy Teenie
Weenie Yellow Polka
Dot Bikini'
by Bombalurina;
'The Twang's The Thang'
by Duane Eddy;
The South Pacific
soundtrack was at No. 1
in the album charts at
the start of April 1960
— by the end of the
month, *The Sound of
Music* hit the top spot.

Also in 1960:
Record Retailer (later
to become *Music Week*)
publishes the first
UK album chart;
The contraceptive pill;
President Kennedy
takes power in the
United States;
Heart Pacemakers;
Felt tip pens;
Drinks in aluminium cans;
Nuclear aircraft
carriers;
Weather satellites;
Protest sit-ins;
D. H. Lawrence's *Lady
Chatterley's Lover*;
Hitchcock's *Psycho*.

"I'm happy new life's been injected into the boot, but I don't really keep up any more - I'm more interested in my oils, my cars and my country patients."

Dr. Maertens speaking in 1988.

"Mr Ray Griggs said that there is no end to the types of footwear that can be produced. Great interest was being shown, business taken so far was substantial and prospects appeared to be bright...the shoes were most comfortable to wear and gave the impression of walking on air."

An extract from *Shoe & Leather News*, June 16th, 1960

Function before Fashion

'Serious Injury Avoided.'

Mr Joseph Baker of Newcastle Upon Tyne has good reason to be thankful for having worn boots by R. Griggs and Co. A stone of about 6ft by 3ft fell on his shoulder and foot. Whilst his shoulder required profuse stitching, his foot only suffered a blackened toenail.

Extract from *Shoe & Leather News*

"It's a fact! The working man has never before been offered a really comfortable boot. Hard work - hard boots had to be accepted. The revolutionary Dr. Martens Air Cushioned soles puts an end to this foot-breaking torture...a most pleasant experience for the much abused foot."

Advert for Doc Martens, 1960

In the first few years of the '60s, sales of DM's were almost exclusively provided by postmen, factory workers, builders, policemen, medics, Underground staff and other workers. Costing just £2 on their launch, the boots were soon complemented by the three hole plain Derby shoe, the 1461. This proved particularly popular with the Post Office, who have continually utilised Dr. Martens shoes. The boot was popular with the police, although it was not until the late '70s that Docs were cited as standard uniform - although some specified that the trademark yellow stitching had to be penned in black to meet colour regulations. The soles, which were resistant to oil, petrol and acid, proved particularly useful for dealing with leaking car fuel at the scene of traffic accidents. Other officers said the soft soles proved invaluable for sneaking up on criminals, whilst the high legged quarters offered extra protection against attack.

Possibly the first public figure to consistently wear Dr. Martens was Tony Benn. Born Anthony Wedgewood Benn, this socialist MP was actually a Viscount - Viscount Stangate - but championed workers' rights and other related issues. He would often march at the front of CND protests in his cloth button-down shirts and grey suits, complete with black 1461 shoes. It was a style that was copied in later years by figures from across the political spectrum - Trotskyist lecturers and Socialist Worker students often wore Docs, possibly as a sign of political alignment with the workers they campaigned for, who trudged to their job each day in the very same boots.

At this point, Doc Martens seemed a highly unlikely fashion item, despite the fact that boots were involved in fashion like never before - the stylish Chelsea boot, the cuban heeled Beatle boot of Fab Four fame, the Clarks desert boot and the so-called knee-high kinky boot were all very popular. Even the ladies ankle boot, based on a style from the 1800s, had made a comeback. A rash of other footwear had also recently merged including loafers, sandals and chisel toes. Form was placed most definitely before function.

Moreover, England, and in particular London, had replaced Paris as the fashion capital of the world. The gaudy colours of Carnaby Street ruled the day and international magazines such as *Time* hailed the merits of 'Swinging London', as both sides of the Atlantic headed for the late '60s and the psychedelic trip of the 'Summer of Love.'

Fortunately, the rather clumpy Doc Martens continued to sell in increasing quantities to workers - after all, such a boot was surely never going to find its way into the world of fashion...

"Sex began in 1963."
Poet Philip Larkin.

`Also in the early '60s:`
`Valium arrives;`
`Russia's Yuri Gagarin`
`becomes the first`
`man in space;`
`Cassette recorder`
`invented;`
`Lung transplants.`

In the mid-1600s, Oliver Cromwell had marched into Wellingborough and demanded 20,000 pairs of boots for his Ironside soldiers, thus creating the shoe trade in Northamptonshire county. The county's hardworking cobblers were soon drinking in taverns called The Boot Inn, or the Cedric Arms, so named after the patron Saint of shoemakers.

Singer-songwriter Billy Bragg with Tony Benn, outside the House of Commons' statue of Oliver Cromwell

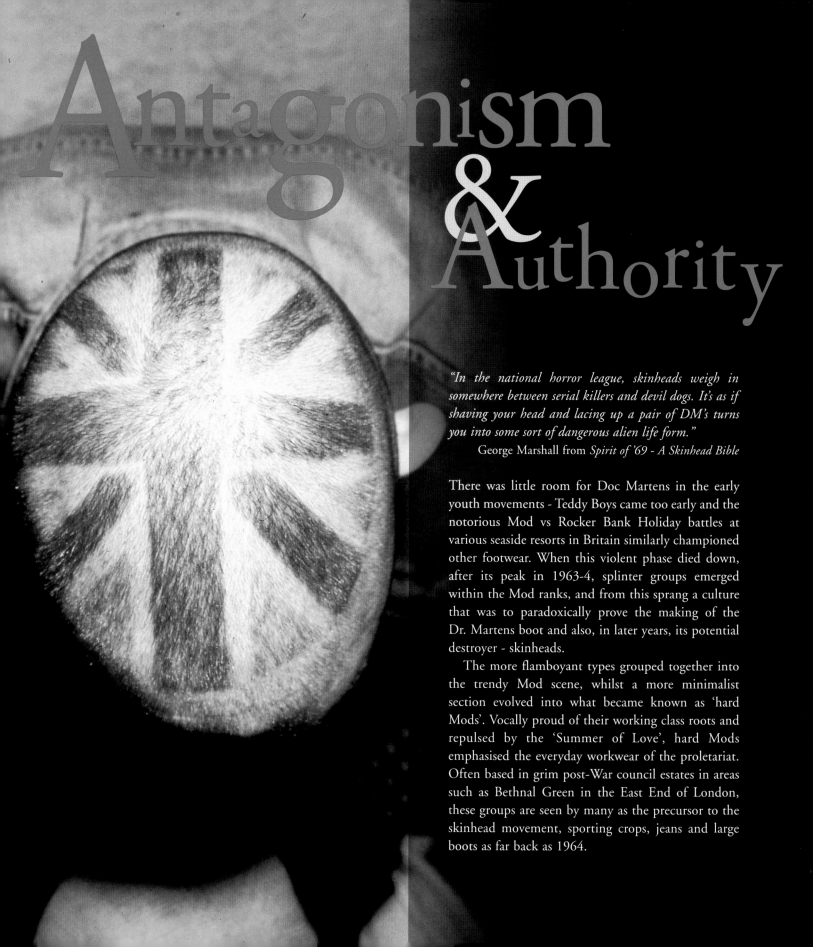

Antagonism & Authority

"In the national horror league, skinheads weigh in somewhere between serial killers and devil dogs. It's as if shaving your head and lacing up a pair of DM's turns you into some sort of dangerous alien life form."

George Marshall from *Spirit of '69 - A Skinhead Bible*

There was little room for Doc Martens in the early youth movements - Teddy Boys came too early and the notorious Mod vs Rocker Bank Holiday battles at various seaside resorts in Britain similarly championed other footwear. When this violent phase died down, after its peak in 1963-4, splinter groups emerged within the Mod ranks, and from this sprang a culture that was to paradoxically prove the making of the Dr. Martens boot and also, in later years, its potential destroyer - skinheads.

The more flamboyant types grouped together into the trendy Mod scene, whilst a more minimalist section evolved into what became known as 'hard Mods'. Vocally proud of their working class roots and repulsed by the 'Summer of Love', hard Mods emphasised the everyday workwear of the proletariat. Often based in grim post-War council estates in areas such as Bethnal Green in the East End of London, these groups are seen by many as the precursor to the skinhead movement, sporting crops, jeans and large boots as far back as 1964.

They listened to soul and Jamaican ska, with Brixton and Lambeth parties introducing them both to new music as well as the highly influential Kingston Rude boy scene that had migrated from the Caribbean with young Jamaicans. Also prevalent at this time was the terrace bootboy, and it was a combination of these three disparate cultures that merged to form the skinhead movement.

One of the first instances of recognisable skinheads appearing in public came during the Great Vietnam Solidarity March in London, 1968, when 30,000 students were heckled by 200 or so closely cropped local youths in Millwall football club team colours.

Interestingly, at this early stage, the haircut was less important than the heavy boots, which were the defining item of clothing. Docs were hardly used at all in the initial stages - instead, National Coal Board miners' boots or army boots were popular, usually with no more than eight or nine holes. It was not until the skinheads picked up on the Dr. Martens boot that its place in modern subculture began. Dr. Martens didn't become popular until their steel toe-capped predecessors (which in a few instances had spikes welded on to them) were classed as 'offensive weapons' by the football police and instantly confiscated. This led to Docs quickly becoming almost standard issue for the skinhead, with some wearing them several sizes too big to exaggerate their presence. The boots had that appealing uniformity of look for the average skinhead who craved this gang mentality. Also, their simple utilitarian design was both an anti-fashion statement and a nod to their working class roots, a badge of both power and pride.

The simple appeal of being very comfortable also sold them to the skinheads, plus the fact that they polished up better than any rival boot. This is one element of skinheads that is often overlooked - the attention to detail in their presentation, a characteristic inherited from the Mods. As they needed no time to style their hair, skins spent hours on their clothes and footwear, polishing their DM's almost obsessively. One peculiar trend was to 'antique' the boots. This involved polishing a pair of cherry reds with black shoe polish, which was then rubbed off, leaving rivulets of black in the creases. Skins also used a repair called 'hot-knifing', whereby the heated blade is inserted into the split sole and pressed back on to the upper (a tip actually described in Dr. Martens' early in-box literature).

'Bovver Boys' is taken from the slang euphemism of 'bother', as skins would often go out 'looking for bother.'

This is indicative of the fact that for many people, not just skins, DM's are worn in rather than wearing out, and great sentimental affection is held for each pair. They gain more character and improve with age.

The rest of the skinhead look was uncompromisingly working class, reactionary even. When set against the flamboyant flower power culture and high fashion of the '60s, this was a real counter-culture statement. Trousers were worn short to display the boots, with the long laces often tied through the famous AirWair heel tag. Ben Sherman button-down shirts (at this stage plain - checks didn't appear until the early '70s) with red tag button-fly Levis were the other most popular accoutrements for the skinhead.

Corduroys were also sometimes worn. The Levis were meant to be worn around the hips but skins wore them higher around the waist, thus requiring braces, which varied in width and colours. The best looking jeans were faded, but as the material was so strong, a bottle of bleach was often thrown over them to speed up the effect.

Musically, the early skins were into reggae, soul and ska, and championed artists like Desmond Dekker, Max Romeo and The Pyramids. Many a youth club was filled with black and white kids dancing to the same songs, mixing without a hint of trouble, a fact which makes a mockery of the later racist elements of the skinhead movement. Unfortunately, increasing levels of violence began to turn public opinion against the skinheads.

Like all subcultures, skinhead soon started evolving and fragmenting. One such descendant was the suedehead, a look which began appearing around 1970. These were skins who grew their hair slightly longer, probably to avoid the stigma of being a skinhead. They wore tonic suits and Crombie coats all day and even sometimes carried umbrellas and the occasional bowler hat (umbrella tips were often filed to a sharpe point and then re-painted black). So-called because of their hairstyle, which they preened with steel combs, suedeheads tended to wear patterned brogues (known as Royals) rather than Docs. The boots were too hard, too military in appearance and hence largely shunned, as indeed they were by the next skinhead hybrid, the short-lived smoothies.

By 1972, the first wave of skinhead was effectively over. The violence, the anti-social image and changing fashions had rendered much of their potency redundant. For the Doc Martens boot however, their impact had been undeniably massive - wrenched unwittingly from the workplace, the boot was suddenly popular currency in the subculture of Britain's youth. Despite the latter-day negative repercussions the boot would suffer as a result of its associations with skinheads, their role in its success cannot be under-rated. This, combined with the DM's working class roots, its durability and apparent flexibility to change, meant that the boot was already on its way to becoming a subcultural icon.

The Pyramids recorded the famous 'Skinhead Moonstomp' under the pseudonym of Symarip. The B-side, 'Skinhead Jamboree', hails the skinhead uniform in its lyrics, mentioning both Doc Martens and Levis.

In 1969, Labour Prime Minister Harold Wilson berated some Tory rivals as 'the skinheads of Surbiton.'

Although skinheads were around in some forms as early as 1964, the term was not actually crystallised until the end of the decade. Other early names included cropheads, lemons, no-heads, baldheads, prickles, spy kids and boiled eggs. Most inappropriate of all perhaps was peanuts, said to be used because the engines of skinheads scooters (stripped down practical versions of their Mod forefathers extravagant machines) made a sound like a peanut rattling in a tin.

> "The sight of cropped heads and the sound of heavy boots is cause for sinking feelings in the pit of the stomach."

Chris Welch, *Melody Maker*, 1969

The first book on the subject is widely regarded as Richard Allen's *Skinhead*. Writing under this pseudonym, James Moffat created the most famous skinhead of all-time, Joe Hawkins, who was racist, sexist and violent - the books sold several million copies. Moffat, a native of Canada, wrote over 400 pulp fiction novels before his death of cancer in 1993.

The haircut

Contrary to popular belief, the British skinhead is not actually a descendant of the US crew cut, which has no hair at the back and sides, and a longer top crop. Despite this fact, American military leaders were so scared that their English-based servicemen would be mistaken for skinheads whilst off-duty, that they issued a memo allowing them to wear hairpieces. Others have claimed the skinhead cut originated amongst dockers who shaved their heads to prevent hair lice.

Most skinheads vary from number four on the barber's razor to the shortest, number one. Since this allows little room for self-expression, permutations on the hairline are popular - either square cut, rounded or following the natural line. West Indians sometimes shaved a pencil thin parting in the cut (they called their crop a 'skiffle'), and this caught on with UK skins. Some skins wore a so-called 'dark shadow', where the razor was used with no guard. Baldness was not popular. The occasional large sideburns, known as 'mutton chops' were cherished. Skinhead girls wore the feather cut, cropped on top with delicate wisps over the ears, face and neck. This was often accompanied with fish-net stockings, Monkey boots rather than DM's, and short skirts.

Explosion and Subversion

"Rock is very, very important and very, very ridiculous."

Pete Townshend 199

Pete Townshend of The Who was one of the first high profile people to wear Dr. Martens. Set against a decade of flowery, effeminate styles, Townshend's choice of Dr. Martens was a beacon of austere style. Due to The Who's volatile live show and his characteristic guitar jumps and kicks, the boots were captured in scores of pictures, one of the finest examples of which is this Pennie Smith shot. Townshend even wrote about the boots in his song 'Uniform.'

The Who's place in modern subculture, despite their later status as stadium rock gods, is secure. Their seminal 'My Generation' single quickly saw the band, and songwriter Townshend in particular, being hailed as spokesmen for the day's youth. The song's stuttering speed-fuelled lyrics and brilliant instrumentation (including one of the greatest bass solos of all time, courtesy of John Entwistle) secured The Who a place in rock history on both sides of the Atlantic. This was just one of dozens of classic Who tracks, described by Townshend himself as "sweet songs sung by a violent group."

Their aggressive live show also attracted much attention, not just for the spectacle but also because it horrified the establishment. The band's genius drummer, Keith Moon, often had to tie his drum kit together with rope as he hit the skins so hard. Considered by many to be the greatest rock drummer of all time, 'Moon the Loon', as he was nicknamed, was a whirlwind of energy at the back of the stage. Whilst John Entwistle provided the solitary calm exception in front of him, Daltrey and Townshend were frenetic. The guitarist's windmilling arms bashed away at his bruised strings, often climaxing in the guitar neck being punched through the speakers or simply smashed into pieces on the floor.

When Townshend first met Roger Daltrey he told him he had "been buggering about on guitar for years getting nowhere." This was typical of the many brilliant, unpredictable and frequently acerbic one-liners that Townshend fed to the media over the years, which helped fuel his reputation as one of rock's most articulate, inspired and inspiring forefathers.

The Who's links with Dr. Martens went past Townshend's own preferences. Their superb 1969 rock opera double album *Tommy* was described by some critics as "the most important and innovative rock album since *Sgt. Pepper*." In 1975, Ken Russell turned the opus into a film, and during the performance of the classic 'Pinball Wizard' Elton John narrates the story of the deaf, dumb and blind kid standing atop an enormous pair of brown Dr. Martens. The boots were made of fibreglass and stood 54 inches tall - Elton's size four feet were fitted into another pair of shoes which were strapped on top of the towering twelve holers - Elton kept the boots afterwards. In 1988, at a London auction of rock 'n' roll memorabilia, the current Chairman of AirWair, Stephen Griggs, bought the boots for £12,100 (the event was sparked by Elton wanting to clear out some rooms to redecorate - it raised over £4 million). The over-sized DM's now stand proud in a glass showcase at Northampton's shoe museum.

Pete Townshend is alleged to have done the briefest rock interview of all time, with Rolling Stone *magazine's Cameron Crowe: "I've changed my mind."*

Pete Townshend

When Decca was handed the initial master tape of the seminal 'My Generation' single, they refused to accept it, complaining that the feedback at the end of the track was unplanned distortion. This was only moderately less embarrassing than EMI, who turned The Who down completely.

The Who's contributions to films didn't stop at *Tommy*. Their much-anticipated 1973 double concept album, *Quadrophenia,* became a cult classic when the big screen movie version was released six years later - it is seen by many as one of the best British films ever made. The setting was 1964, the peak of the Mod-Rocker battles. The story told the tale of the young Mod, Jimmy, played by Phil Daniels, who was struggling to assert himself amidst a mess of girls, drugs, violence and growing up. He rides around on his beloved scooter, talks about and tries to sleep with girls, takes copious amounts of uppers and downers, ending up in jail for his troubles. Jimmy wrote himself into Mod legend when he finally cracked and drove his scooter over some cliffs.

Interestingly, The Who had deliberately excluded themselves from the film to reduce its appeal to mainstream America. Instead a relatively unknown cast was chosen. Even Sting, who had two lines as the moody but cool Ace Face, was only just coming to prominence as lead singer of The Police. *Quadrophenia's* broad Cockney accents, the highly stylised clothes, the soundtrack, the association with The Who and the brilliant script made

the film a classic almost immediately. Jimmy the Mod doesn't actually wear Docs in the film, nor do they appear on anyone else, but the scooter and Mod revival provoked by the movie's release saw the boots being worn by an entirely new generation. These scooterboys bought cherry reds in their thousands, wearing them with their distinctive green parkas and an artificial fur tail flying from their heavily mirrored scooters.

Jimmy's complex and endearing character was said to be made up of all four of The Who's personalities - the meaning of the word 'quadrophenia.'

Phil Daniels later became a Royal Shakespeare actor - he appeared in an RSC performance of Clockwork Orange. *He even formed a band of his own, called Phil Daniels and the Cross, who released one eponymously titled album. He also went on to make a cameo appearance on Blur's hit single 'Parklife'.*

Mods themselves did not generally wear Docs - the late '70s stereotype is associated much more with the black and white bowling shoe as worn by The Jam. This modernist movement started off as a secretive working class cult in the clubs and cafés of Soho and west London in the late '50s, surfacing publicly around 1962. The original Mod look was cosmopolitan: Italian suits, French hair cuts, British shirts. They had historical blood brothers in America's Cool School Jazz men and Italy's so-called *pavoneggiarsi,* but it was the British Mod who crystallised the trend.

The Who themselves enjoyed a considerable Mod following, despite the fact that their own Mod incarnation as The High Numbers and the subsequent single, 'I'm The Face', was a flop.

Elton John's boots as worn in Tommy

QUADROPHENIA

Clockwork Orange addicts

A Vicious Strangeness

In 1971, Stanley Kubrick's highly controversial film *Clockwork Orange* was released to both underground acclaim and mainstream outrage. Based on the Anthony Burgess book of the same name, the film centred around the character of Alex Delarge (played by Malcolm McDowell), a gang leader whose violent life leads to a prison term, which he is released from on condition he undergoes a 'cure for criminals.' This involves mind-altering drugs which create nausea and illness if the subject thinks of sex or violence and anti-social behaviour. This invasion of his civil liberties, set against the backdrop of his gang's own dark, depraved activities, created a compelling paradox. The inclusion of the film's own vocabulary - the gang members were called 'droogs', the language itself named 'nadsat', being half-Cockney, half-Russian - added to its allure, as did the affront caused by the 'ultra-violence', namely graphic acts of barbarity, including sexual attacks. This hard edge, the brutal subtext and the highly stylised art direction gave *Clockwork Orange* all the trappings of a cult classic.

When the film was withdrawn from circulation after a 61 week run, its status as a taboo yet acclaimed masterpiece was assured. In the immediate aftermath, some youths started wearing the distinctive white outfits, black bowler hats and clumpy boots, a hybrid of city gent style and bootboy intimidation. Others perpetrated copycat acts of violence, which a headline hungry media instantly labelled 'clockwork crimes.' The banning of the film meant poor quality pirate videos quickly started to spring up in backstreets, only adding to its appeal.

Ironically, the large black boots that feature so heavily in the film are not actually Dr. Martens. However, in the aftermath of its release, those who chose to follow and mimic the style tended to wear DM's. A crossover with musical subcultures existed as always, with several bands drawing directly on the film. Major Accident, The Violators, Blitz and The Clockwork Soldiers all openly admired Kubrick's work, whilst California's Durango 95 took their name from the car driven by the droogs. The Adicts were perhaps the biggest fans, with lead singer Monkey dressing up entirely as a Clockwork skin and aping Alex Delarge's disconcerting grin to perfection. Their album artwork also depicted scenes from the film.

Clockwork Orange remains banned.

Tribal Trappings

The early '70s saw the first pairs of painted Docs on these football terraces. Team colours were most popular, although white was also prevalent. Steel toe-caps were frequently exposed for extra menace and these were the preferred weapon of abuse. As mentioned above, police forces across the country quickly declared such boots 'an offensive weapon.' In response, non-steel toe-caps became popular, which meant Dr. Martens sold heavily.

Public outrage at this violence was rabid - some **critics** argued that the **hooligans** should be **torched** with a flame-thrower.

Tabloid clippings of football fans removing their boots and laces on match-day

Even without steel toe-caps, DM's could still wreak substantial damage, so the police developed a new tactic. They made anyone wearing Docs remove their laces, the theory being that much less harm could be done with a loose boot, and terrace charges were rendered virtually impossible. The fans quickly counter-acted this by smuggling spare sets of laces in their trousers. Police spotted this and banned shops in the locality from selling laces on match days - in response, the hooligans would thread paper clips or wire into their jacket linings. Sometimes, girlfriends were enlisted to smuggle things into stadiums, as they were less likely to be searched. With no option left, the police introduced the ultimate deterrent, forcing fans to take their boots off completely. They then stood guard over these bare-footed hordes until the opposition fans had left for home. After that, a massive free-for-all would ensue as people tried to reclaim their own boots - and sometimes a newer pair of someone else's.

In keeping with the boots' rather unsavoury early history, the menace of football hooliganism also found a place for Dr. Martens. There are many theories as to when this phenomenon started, but the general consensus is that the 1968-69 season was a watershed, with aggressive skinhead mobs prowling the terraces. In the wake of England's 1966 World Cup triumph, attendances at soccer matches were at record levels - the buoyant employment market created a swathe of affluent youth who started travelling to matches away from home. With this more territorial activity, which coincided with a renewed patriotism courtesy of the government's 'I'm Backing Britain' campaign, violence started increasing. The football firm was born.

Despite their aggressive intentions, there were still interesting stylistic characteristics to these groups - they were the epitome of terrace fashion. Some wore white butcher's coats with team names across the back - the so-called 'Chelsea Headhunters' firm even splattered their coats with blood for extra authenticity. Others dressed as droogs from *Clockwork Orange*.

It wasn't just the Dr. Martens boot that was used - a veritable arsenal of weaponry found its way on to the terraces - bottles, blades, darts, razors in oranges, throwing stars, lead piping and even a 'Millwall brick' - a newspaper rolled up so tightly it formed a thick, hard club. Small coins and paper were often improvised to form impromptu knuckle-dusters.

When police started separating opposition fans inside the ground, the violence only spread outside to railway stations, trains, cafes, pubs, anywhere. Indeed, one of the most famous firms of all, West Ham's ICF, travelled exclusively on Inter City trains, hence their name: Inter City Firm. Other notorious firms included Portsmouth's 6.57 Crew, the Chelsea Headhunters and the Millwall Bushwackers.

When Prince Charles and Lady Diana were married in 1981, some 750 million viewers worldwide tuned it to watch. The highlight of the ceremony for many was when the BBC's overhead helicopter flew past a multi-storey car park, on whose roof were the words 'All the best to Chas and Di from West Ham Skins.'

Current President of AirWair, Max Griggs' passion for football has seen him involved in Rushden & Diamonds soccer team, as well as Dr. Martens sponsoring West Ham United.

Until recently, Max Griggs knew all of his employees by name.

The '70s was notable in many ways for the fact that the UK and the US music scene moved in largely different directions. After the demise of the Beatles, the US went for the heavier rock of Led Zeppelin as well as other stadium bands such as Crosby, Stills and Nash and The Who. The UK however plumped for glam rock, with Bowie, Bolan, The Sweet, Slade, and Roxy Music leading the way. Unfortunately, the decade started with the deaths of several of rock's leading lights - Jimi Hendrix, Janis Joplin and Jim Morrison. However, from this bleak beginning grew some inspiring and at times revolutionary music - and DM's played a part in much of that.

Spiders and Sequins

Although not readily associated with the outrageous fashions of glam rock, the Dr. Martens boot did find a place in certain areas of this most extravagant of subcultures. The first genuine British skinhead band were Slade, who went on to develop a glam rock image and reap the benefits with scores of hits, including 'Mama Weer Al Crazee Now' and 'Cum On Feel The Noize.'

In 1969, when skinheads were first starting to come to public prominence, a long-haired Slade were playing a four month residency in the Bahamas as a reggae and soul backing band. Yet, as the cover of their debut album, *Play It Loud,* showed, they were about to undergo a dramatic image change that lasted for three years. Lead singer Noddy Holder picks up the story: "We were looking for an image that would set us apart in the clubs and ballrooms. At this stage, skinhead was far more about fashion than any politics. We were working class lads from the Black Country, and so the street look came fairly naturally to us. Adopting that skinhead look gained us overnight recognition - suddenly, everyone knew it was Slade."

Noddy Holder

N O D D Y

"We had no problem getting live gigs in the early days - even the Universities who didn't like the skinhead look still booked us because we were a great live band. Most skinheads were into reggae and ska but we played more soul in a rock vein, even some Motown classics. Skins never adopted us solely as their band, so our audiences were always very mixed. The image worked very well for live shows but TV and radio didn't give us much work - the producers were frightened of us. So after a while we started to change. We didn't ditch the skinhead look entirely though - we kept the short trousers but made them far more colourful. We also kept the hair essentially short but grew it very long at the back. At this point, it wasn't called glam rock and there was really only us and Marc Bolan doing this stuff. When we did return to skinhead clubs, they were flabbergasted!"

In his book, The Sex Life of the Foot And Shoe, *William Rossi argues that the '70s platform boot was so asexual that it caused a decline in the birthrate, due to a lack of desire between the sexes.*

"I had my **hair** cut in London and I was living with my **Mom**. Our **manager** Chas Chandler took us to get our crops done by the **bloke** who gave Jimi Hendrix his wildman look.

We bought the **Docs** from an Army & Navy store and went back to my Mother's at **4am**. She hadn't seen me for a few days and when she came in the **next morning** to wake me up, all she could see was this **great big pair** of Dr. Martens at the end of my bed and my **bald head!** She freaked out! My mates called me The Pinkhead or **Don the Blue Head.**"

Noddy Holder

At this point, 90% of Docs were still the eight hole originals, with three hole shoes filling the rest of the market. Cherry red and black were the only two colours available. As a result, DM's struggled against the lurid spectacle that was glam rock. Knee-high platform boots were frequently covered in glitter, and sometimes painted with flowers - a precursor to the later DM's fashion in the '80s and '90s.

Those glam kids who did customise their Docs often used bicycle spray paint, as this had metallic glitter in it.

Thigh high boots were originally worn by pirates and smugglers because they could easily hide stolen and smuggled valuables in them - hence they were called 'bootleggers', a term still used today.

Fans of the teeny bop sensations the Bay City Rollers wore eight hole Docs along with their tartan scarfs which dangled from their teenage wrists.

Also in 1971: The microprocessor is introduced — a computer on a chip, its inventors promise it will revolutionise the world. Most people are doubtful.

Reasons to be Cheerful, Part 2

Whilst most of Britain was about to be caught up in the wave of bondage trousers that was to become punk, a 35 year old musician from Upminster, Essex was writing brilliantly witty, sensitive and musically gifted songs - Ian Dury. One of rock music's great characters, Dury was stricken by polio at the age of seven but proved to be academically talented and went on to teach art until he was 28. At the beginning of the '70s he started playing the pub circuit in London with his band Kilburn and the High Roads, mastering old R&B classics and injecting them with his own brand of incisive and insightful lyrics, usually semi-spoken in his inimitable Cockney slang. By 1975, he was at the heart of the pub rock scene.

"...t **four** years ago I gave a pair of **Martens** to a mate of mine, **the Skunk**. He's dead no... said to me, 'Are these the **originals** on the front of *New Boots and Panties*?' I said 'No,' but he wa... a letter of **authentication** to **auction** them at Christies. I gave him... **letter,** but he didn't quite pull it off."

Pub rock was a fairly lonely beacon of integrity amidst a mid-70s scene awash with bloated mega-groups and corporate, cocaine-snorting rock. On both sides of the Atlantic, prolonged and tiresome prog rock and AOR was ruling the charts and the airwaves. Even The Who's *Tommy* was seen by many critics as part of this narcissistic scene, and cited as an example of music losing its way. Pub rock was the first reaction against such decadence and the precursor to punk. Other groups who featured in this scene were Brinsley Schwarz, Dr. Feelgood and Bees Make Honey. They played R&B covers and back-to-basics blues mixed with some original material, and deliberately performed in small venues, with Islington's Hope & Anchor pub being the key London gig.

Ian Dury's critically acclaimed solo album, *New Boots and Panties*, saw him recognised as one of the country's most original songwriters – the album spent a year in the charts. Dury later went on to enjoy a No. 1 single with 'Hit Me With Your Rhythm Stick' with his band the Blockheads. In the late '80s he turned to acting and wrote a ...sical called *Apples*. He remains one of Britain's most gifted and...

Dury was an unusual bedfellow to a mass o... progressives, left-wing students and art schoo... types who adopted Dr. Martens as their own in th... middle of this decade. Sales of the 1460 still rulec... but the shoe version was blossoming, and seemec... to be edging its way into the psyche of politics and... alternative thought, despite its close proximity to... the much-maligned skinhead movement. Indeed... its establishment as the left-winger's footwear o... choice meant that from this point onwards, man... a Doc-clad skinhead rally would clash with horde... of Anti-Nazi campaigners or socialist protesters... both dressed dramatically differently, except fo... one thing - their choice of footwear.

Ian Dury once called Dr. Martens 'a communisti... shoe' because of its mass produced nature mixed wit... its ability to allow individuality. The boot can indee...

History is made by

1976 was an eventful year in many ways. Concorde made its first supersonic commercial flight, Mao Zedong died and Apple Computers was formed by Steven Jobs and Stephen Wozniak. The dictionary opened its arms to two new words - junk food and sound-bite. NASA's Viking 1 probe beamed back the first ever pictures of the surface of Mars, and an earthquake in Tangshan, China, the biggest of the century, killed 250,000 people.

Back in Britain it was the driest summer since 1727 and, faced with growing political divisions within his cabinet and domestic unrest, Harold Wilson quit as Prime Minister, suffering a severe leadership defeat shortly after at the hands of James Callaghan. Elsewhere, things were even worse - Jim Reeves and Perry Como had been fighting it out for the No. 1 slot in the album charts. Not for long.

The history books tell us that punk broke in 1976, but it was actually at the tail end of 1975, 6th November, to be precise. An irate manager of a tiny upstairs room at St. Martin's School of Art thought that the band he had booked, the Sex Pistols, were so noisey he had to cut the power after only five songs. Eight months later and that same band had re-ignited this most incendiary of art forms.

In doing so, the Sex Pistols inspired, and were in turn inspired by, hordes of artists, singers, designers, and other cultural experimentalists. The most direct legacy of punk, obviously, was the music. Two young northern Grammar school boys were watching the Pistols at High Wycombe in early 1976, then drove home to Manchester afterwards vowing to form their own band. Taking their name from a headline in *Time Out* magazine, Pete Shelley and Howard Devoto formed Buzzcocks, whose brand of abrasive melodic pop introduced the world to such pop classics as 'Ever Fallen In Love With Someone You Shouldn't

Have Fallen In Love With?' They also formed their own record label, New Hormones, which has since been credited with being the first 'indie' record company. When Buzzcocks debuted in Manchester, supporting their heroes the Pistols, the crowd was small but enthusiastic, and contained amongst others Ian Curtis, Bernard Sumner and Peter Hook, later of Joy Division, Tony Wilson (who would later form Factory Records) and Steven Patrick Morrissey.

By mid-76, punk was gathering momentum, and with a headline-hungry media sniffing around the seedy clubs and sweaty gigs of the punk circuit, things started to happen. The first punk record was The Damned's 'New Rose', just pipping the Pistols' 'Anarchy In The UK' by a few weeks.

On the gig circuit, things were far more active. The now-legendary 100 Club Punk Festival in London's Oxford Street on 20th and 21st September, saw a first night bill including the Sex Pistols, Subway Sect and Siouxsie and the Banshees - the following night saw the likes of The Damned, the Vibrators, and Buzzcocks. The two night event was infamous for many reasons - Sid Vicious, a member of the so-called Bromley Contingent, played drums for the hastily formed Siouxsie and the Banshees, and some observers claimed that he also invented 'the pogo' that night, violently jumping up and down to the thrashed guitars. He also smashed a beer glass against a pillar, allegedly blinding a girl in one eye.

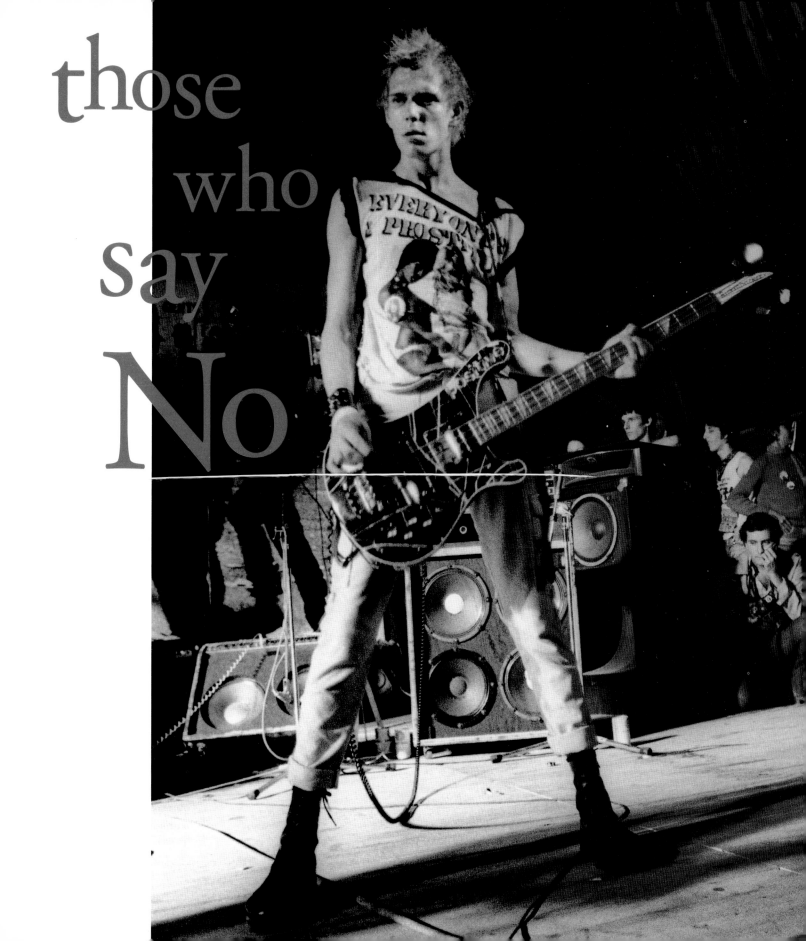

those who say No

The tabloid frenzy against this violence raised punk's profile another notch, but this was negligible compared to the furore that followed the so-called 'Bill Grundy incident', when the Pistols swore on the early evening *Today* show. The public reacted by jamming the television station's switchboard with complaints and the following morning's *Daily Mirror* front page denounced this latest group with the line, 'The Filth and the Fury' (ironically, the Sex Pistols were famous for *not* wearing Dr. Martens, instead preferring brothel creepers and biker boots or even trainers).

Despite the fact that punks were actually doing much the same as all the teenagers before them - upsetting the older generation - it was not essentially what they did that made the headlines so powerful but the public's rabid reactions. The establishment's horror merely reinforced the counter-culture potency of the movement.

J. J. Burnel of The Stranglers

Catwoman

"**Punk** is a **symptom** of the way society is **declining**. It could have a **shocking effect** on young people."

A British politician and punk critic, 1977

The floodgates of punk now opened. It was no longer the preserve of the London in-crowd. Suddenly, the provincial kid could also be a part of something his parents detested. Musically, there was little to tempt Britain's youth away from the bulging wave of snarling punk venom - The Eagles had become the first group to achieve platinum status with their *Greatest Hits 1971-75* album, whilst the likes of Brotherhood of Man and Showaddywaddy dominated the charts.

Punks quickly established their own identity. Individuality was the key, with hand-sprayed clothes, ripped trousers and extravagant hairstyles. In London, bondage trousers were one of the staple items of punk's stereotypical look, and a select few punk clothing shops offered an array of weird and wonderful items. In the provinces, improvisation introduced crudely painted T-shirts, mohair jumpers, and tight trousers. One interesting feature was an occasional trend to misappropriate elements of Teddy Boy fashions, such as the string ties or drainpipe trousers - these items were frequently worn much to the annoyance of the purist Teds.

The availability of punk fashion was extremely limited. Londoners had an elite choice of a handful of shops, but in the provinces, however, there were no such outlets, and kids were forced to plunder Salvation Army and other charity shops for ideas. One item of punk gear that was available on a national scale, however, and at a uniform price, was the Dr. Martens boot.

As such, the black DM's boot became a constant feature of most punk's wardrobes, crammed as they were with thrift shop style. Punk's two defining fashion statements - badly cut short hair and any trousers except flares - helped make the boot uncannily suitable.

"DM's remind me of the Undertones in 1979 - good year, good boots, good drugs."
Alan McGee, owner of Creation Records, home to Oasis, Primal Scream and The Jesus and Mary Chain.

The individuality of punk's ethos filtered into the fashions as well as the music. Just as DIY songwriting was the order of the day, so DIY fashion design prevailed. Irreverent home made T-Shirts were hand-painted or sprayed with provocative slogans, often taken from films or books. Sometimes, deliberately low grade items were chosen, such as string vests which were dyed in bright colours; alternatively, haute couture items such as silk shirts were defaced, slashed or filled with aesthetically placed holes. Safety pins, badges, patches, tape and chains were all improvised to make unique garments. Economy of price and style was vital.

This flexibility of style might have proved debilitating to DM's appeal, but the boot also proved to have scope for change - punk's confidence of spirit saw many Docs quickly and uniquely customised. Malcolm Garrett, who designed all of the Buzzcocks artwork (and along with Jamie Reid became one of the two lynchpins of punk design), recalls vividly embellishing his own pair of 1460's: "I painted my brown pair bright orange and silver, to coincide with the Buzzcocks debut album release *Another Music In A Different Kitchen*. I had designed that album sleeve to be deliberately striking, very simple, clinical even. I wanted my Docs to look the same, but I couldn't find any orange shoe paint so they ended up being red."

In many senses, the Dr. Martens 1460 was anathema to much of what punk fashion stood for - many punks were unique, non-uniform, and so the 1460 was arguably the only item of punk gear that was of a standard design. Up until now, many associated the boot with skinhead culture, so some punks were reluctant to buy them, but its popularity was inevitably reinforced by its durability and look. Of course, there were dozens of other styles of punk footwear, the sling back, the army combat boot, the brothel creeper, the Monkey boot, even plastic jelly sandals and white stilettos. The 1460 was attainable even to the most hard-up of punks, and its hard-wearing longevity provided further economy.

"Those gobbing little shits would hang around trying to blag in for free with fuck all else but boredom to play with. They would devote hours to personal graffitti, painting anarchy symbols on their Docs, brassing the eyelets with nail varnish remover and letting the world know that nothing is permanent."

Rat Scabies of The Damned.

Whenever someone talks about the NEW WAVE they mean the 'new

wave' of music & musicians that have emerged & influenced the
scene in the last two years. The only new wave is in music.
It has succeeded & failed. Succeeded with a reapraisal of the
ideas, aims, & philosophies of a new set of musicians and of
audiences. It failed by our lack to separate the wheat from
the chaf and thinking that one battle wins the war.
The succees is due to action - the failure due to apathy.
One wave does not make much headway headway up the beach.
If the tide is to turn then one wave must be followed by
another and so on until the all cliffs start to crumble.
This is just the new wave of the turning tide. The next wave
will start from where this one has finnished. So don't slacken
off now, but slip into a higher gear. There still is a lot more
we can do.
    The NEW WAVE is not just about music. It is a challenge to
Consider every thing you do,think, and feel. For some it has
meant a change in fashion and in life style. But most of the
fashion has become cliched and most of the groups have even now
become boring old farts future tax exiles and full of crap such
as saying " I don't want to hear about politics, I just want to
have a good time. It's only rock & roll." But it's not only
rock & roll! If it was then what is all the fuss about it?
Politics is people & people is YOU
I'm not on about party politics not the NF or The Tories. I'm
talking about PERSONAL politics. The way that you react to the
people around you. The ways that you love them, fuck them, hate it
them, slate them. Things like love, jealousy, hate, anger, sex ...
How often do you do some thing to some one & not know why you
did it?
    The NEW WAVE is like a spring clean. You were prepared to throw
out the rubbish in your wardrobe and your record collection.
So why not chuck out all the prides & predx prejudices clutter-
ing up your personality????
    Just think about how you react with other people.
    I'll write more when I think of what to say.

This is all I could think of. Keep the new wave NEW.

Pete Shelley

One striking aspect of punk was that despite the undoubted enormous impact it had on fashion, music, culture, business, art and virtually every other aspect of popular culture, within a few months of its demise, it was deemed painfully unfashionable. The clothing, the style, the songs, the behaviour, and the fashions were all discarded abruptly and almost without exception. Indeed, this ruthless slaying of ideas is typical of each new subculture, which has at its heart the rampant desire to destroy the past, in particular the immediate past.

However, one item, more than any other, seemed capable of surviving the demise of the punk phenomenon intact - the Dr. Martens boot.

April 9th, 1977: The Damned become the first British punk band to hit the USA, playing four nights at CBGB's. When they get to their hotel room, they allegedly find several gifts left for them by The Rolling Stones, including a birthday cake and seven meringue pies.

Despite punk being famed for its musical brevity, the record for the shortest track to chart in the US actually pre-dates even Dr. Martens. In 1959, 'Some Kinda Earthquake' by Duane Eddy hit the Top 40, despite being an instrumental lasting only 77 seconds.

"If anyone gives you criticism that starts off 'you should' or 'you shouldn't', walk away immediately."

Paul Westerberg of the Replacements 1995.

Notably, although the United States in many senses boasted as fertile and creative a punk scene as in the UK, the economy and society across the Atlantic was not as fractured as in the UK, and therefore punk initially had far less impact than it did in its native country.

The ClaSh

"There's a million reasons why hippies failed."
Joe Strummer

For many, the greatest punk band of all time is The Clash - more intriguing, more thoughtful and more complex than much of punk's head-down thrash. They were fronted by the enigmatic and inspiring Joe Strummer, the son of a British ambassador to Turkey, where he was born. He was recruited into The Clash by Mick Jones and Paul Simonon after they saw a gig by his pub rock band the 101'ers. The Clash's eponymously titled debut album was recorded in just three weekends (and heavily championed by John Peel). *Rolling Stone* went on to call it 'the definitive punk album.' As the band evolved and punk's sharp edge faded, The Clash began to filter reggae into their sound and an anti-racist rhetoric into their political stance. Their brilliant *London Calling* album broke through in the States where they played to massive arenas nationwide - they later went on to support The Who around the US. After their split in the mid-80s, Strummer went on to work in films, including the soundtrack for *Sid And Nancy*, starring Gary Oldman.

Famous for their black ten hole DM's, The Clash's style was as varied as their music. Their famous spray-painted boiler suits and shirts were mixed with jackets and ties, T-shirts, black leather jackets, black shirts (often sleeveless) and even dog tags.

The Mohawks

were an Indian tribe from Iroquois in New York State; the Mohicans, originally spelt Mohegan, were from Connecticut. Most frequently worn by the Omaha and Osage tribes, the long thin plume of hair represented a line of buffaloes outlined against the horizon at sunset.

The Indians wore their Mohican haircuts as acts of defiance, daring the enemy into attacking them, trying to take their scalp in the process. Their locks were often stiffened with bear grease or walnut oil, thus making the hair resemble the horn of a bull.

The earliest known record of the Western world appropriating the Mohican was in France in 1945, when US paratroopers cut their hair in that style as a gesture of solidarity in the face of the forthcoming jump across the Rhine.

In England in the '50s, Mancunian hairdresser George Mason offered a reward of £1 to the first youth who turned up at his salon and requested a 'mohican'. The winner, fifteen year old errand boy John Ross, was asked only to recommend the salon to his friends. He can comfortably claim to have pre-dated such legendary godfathers of punk as Iggy Pop and Johnny Rotten by at least twenty years.

"No other subculture illustrates more clearly the importance of theft and transformation in the development of style than punk. It incorporates conscious reference to the legacy of all preceding subcultures."

Helen Rees

Welcome to the Real World

As punk faded, it threw up various hybrids, including Oi! This mix of skinhead and punk saw mohicans matched with Docs, skin tight trousers, braces and colourful clothing. This fleeting music press-championed scene appeared to offer a new clarion call to Britain's disaffected youth, and was described by some as 'working class punk' or 'real punk'. In the wake of punk becoming commercialised and sterile, certain purists derided bands like the Sex Pistols and The Clash as having lost sight of the original punk ideals. They claimed punk had been filled with middle class opportunists, dropping their h's, buying high street punk clothes and temporarily dying their hair whilst that was the vogue. Instead, a legion of bands, many of whom had been around before, during and after the 1976 explosion of punk, led a fierce and at times brutal new wave of music.

At the forefront of this new, largely London-centric movement were bands like Sham 69, Cock Sparrer, and Slaughter and the Dogs. UK Subs, the Lurkers, the Ruts, and Menace were also lumped in under this banner. Sham 69, led by the enigmatic Jimmy Pursey, were the leaders, and initially tried to heal social divisions with songs like 'If The Kids Are United.' The Business were one of the other leading lights.

This new wave of skinhead-based subculture wore higher Docs, sometimes as much as 22 holes, and cut their trousers even higher to further emphasise the boot. They cut their hair very short, with the dark shadow and number one being dominant. Facial tattoos became popular, often amateurishly scrawled on someone's face with a blunt needle and a bottle of Indian ink (since most professional tattooists refused to do facial work). These new skins carried with them an air of racism, violence and general thuggery which old school skins disliked enormously, not least because it discredited the whole scene. As a result there were several battles between the two groups, including scraps on London's Kings Road with older skins fighting alongside Teds against the new skins fighting alongside punks.

Unfortunately, the Oi! scene quickly became unraveled by growing scenes of violence. Bands found themselves unwittingly supported by increasing numbers of National Front racists who infected gigs with their exaggerated tribalism. Jimmy Pursey was known to be extremely unhappy about this development, and at one Sham 69 gig when skins rioted, he left the stage in tears. The Cockney Rejects attracted many football fans, especially with their Top 30 take on West Ham's anthem 'I'm Forever Blowing Bubbles.' Other Oi! bands suffered a similar fate, including The Last Resort, the Angelic Upstarts, the Exploited, and the UK Subs. This was despite the fact that many inside the scene felt the media over-emphasised this violent minority. A particularly vicious riot at a 4 Skins gig between Asian youths and Oi! followers proved to be the death knell of the phenomenon - by the end of 1981, the violence had superseded the music and the Oi! movement was finished.

Oi! is possibly from the Cockney pronunciation of 'hey.' Others claim it is taken from the Greek word 'oi poloi' meaning 'common people', or more likely from the Cockney Rejects album Oi, Oi, Oi.

At many gigs by Peter and the Test Tube Babies, security demanded that fans take off their DM's altogether, or at least remove the laces, just as the football police had done so a decade earlier.

Too Much Fighting on the Dance Floor

By the close of 1979, punk's incisive edge had been largely blunted. Its death throes spewed up a myriad of musical hybrids and subcultural splinters, some equally potent, some less so. Although punk in its original form was left to dwindle into self-parody, its impact should never be underestimated. For now, however, it was old news and kids were looking elsewhere for their kicks.

For many, this came with the arrival of 2 Tone. The movement found an unlikely home in the grim, grey Midlands city of Coventry, famous for Lady Godiva, bicycles, cars and the ferocious Second World War bombing raids that razed it to the ground. From the post-war rubble sprang up a modern dystopia, intended to revitalise the ravaged city, but which proved to be little more than a series of desolate grey buildings and large, barren housing estates. 1979 added fuel to the fire of the already disaffected youth of the city, with unemployment high and punk's rebellious but wilting chant falling on deaf ears.

One of these suffocated Coventry youths was Jerry Dammers. The son of a clergyman, Dammers had first sung at church choir and was inspired to be in a rock band by seeing a television performance of The Who's 'My Generation.' Dammers studied art and film and immersed himself in soul, funk and reggae legends like Don Drummond, Desmond Dekker and Prince Buster. Then punk arrived in his town and changed everything.

After being thrown out of The Sissy Stone Soul Band for playing keyboards with his elbows (he was encouraged by some punks in the crowd), Dammers formed the Coventry Automatics with Horace Panter, brothers Noel and Lynval Golding and former punks Terry Hall and Roddy 'Radiation' Byers. Legend has it that prior to this, Dammers travelled to London to try to recruit a post-Pistols Johnny Rotten on vocals. Several permutations later and the band's name was eventually changed to The Specials. After dozens of cramped rehearsals in Dammers flat (because his keyboard was too big to go through the doors), the band set about establishing their legend.

Their initial blend of reggae and punk proved unpopular with live audiences. On tour with The Clash, they found themselves the target of many an empty bottle which was flung stagewards (and several full ones). After this demoralising tour, in the cold winter of 1978-9, The Specials began to form their masterplan. They dropped the reggae influence and made a side step to ska - the combination of this rhythmical vibrancy and punk's raw energy proved immediately explosive.

Signing a ground-breaking record deal with Chrysalis, The Specials formed their own record label, 2 Tone, which was to provide the new movement with a spiritual home. London band Madness appeared for one single, (the tribute to ska originator Prince Buster, namely 'The Prince'), and The Specials' own Elvis Costello-produced eponymous debut album gave them a Top 5 hit. 2 Tone would go on to see other releases from bands such as The Swinging Cats, The Friday Club, J.B. Allstars, The Apollinairs, the Bodysnatchers and Elvis Costello himself.

Also in 1979: Sony Walkman; Trivial Pursuit; John Wayne dies; Earl Mountbatten assassinated by IRA; Maggie Thatcher wins election and becomes first European woman ever to hold the highest office.

After **dozens** of **cramped** rehearsals

Jerry Dammers on tour.

in Dammers' **flat**, the band
set about establishing their **legend**.

Other main players in this latest subculture were The Beat, Selecter, and of course Madness. Other non-2 Tone ska acts included The Tigers, Ska City Rockers, The Akrylykz, The Employees, and The Pirahnas. These bands all thrived on the first wave of ska musicians such as the Skatalites, Baba Brooks, Ernest Ranglin, Laurel Aitken, and Desmond Dekker. Indeed, Rico Rodriguez, who played as a session musician in Jamaica and was trained by Dammers' hero Don Drummond, would later go on to guest with The Specials.

Terry Hall and Jerry Dammers

In September 1979, Madness and The Specials toured together and provoked a snowball of media and public interest in the developing new movement. The previously reluctant music press jumped on-board and the exposure proved invaluable. Once 2 Tone was heard nationwide, it literally exploded. Within months, it was *the* scene at schools, youth clubs, gigs, on the streets and in the underground. Later, The Specials' masterpiece, 'Ghost Town', hit No. 1, just as Britain's inner cities ignited in a rash of rioting in Toxteth, Brixton, and Handsworth. The song justifiably became the definitive snapshot of the times. It reflected the desperation of inner city life, the poverty of some people in early Thatcherite Britain, and the dissatisfaction and frustration of the sections of society that were being ostracised by the Iron Lady.

This anti-establishment feel appealed to many in the skinhead movement and drew them into 2 Tone. Ska picked up on elements of the Mod revival as well, and so the crowds at these gigs were an eclectic and thoroughly varied mix - black rudeboys, white skinheads, Mods, punks and suedeheads. This anti-racist element was a key factor - some fascist groups often incited fights at ska gigs and The Specials' tour bus was once bricked as it drove past some neo-Nazis. As a retort to this, Dammers and many of the key figures of the scene became involved in ideas such as Rock Against Racism, and later the Nelson Mandela Freedom Campaign. Dammers himself had experienced this scourge at first hand - an Asian Doctor was stabbed to death in a chip shop opposite his flat.

As with all musical or cultural movements, 2 Tone had its very own distinct dress code. The origins of this were embedded deep in Jamaica with the rude boy culture of the late '50s. 'Rude boy' was a term for the subculture of frustrated, unemployed and often violent youths who roamed the dancehalls earning an anti-social reputation in the newly independent Jamaica. Some felt this was justified, others saw the Rude boys as unfairly derogated - *Melody Maker* once called them 'cool super-hooligans.' Jimmy Cliff played just such a rude boy, Ivanhoe Martin Rhygin', in the Perry Hanzell film, *The Harder They Come*, a classic ska movie. This culture drew heavily on a mixture of imported American R&B and jazz, mixed with various African cultures.

Rude boys took great pride in their fashionable attire - extremely neat suits were made by backstreet tailors with noticeably short trousers, usually in two tone fabrics. The outfits were completed with loafers and optional pork pie hats, sometimes called 'stingy brims' or 'bluebeat hats.' When Desmond Dekker first came to the UK, his record company bought him a suit - he immediately took a pair of scissors and cut off the bottom six inches of each trouser leg.

This fascinating backdrop was 2 Tone's inspiration. This newer version was racially liberal, fun-loving and stylistically as much in debt to elements of Mod culture as Jamaican fashion. The hats, dark suits and narrow ties did translate from Jamaica however. Early Rude boys almost without exception wore loafers, usually black, and their shirts and hats were often far more colourful than the later monochrome style. This was a direct descendant of the extravagant tailoring of the Jamaicans, and was predictably toned down for the British equivalent, not least because they would be off-the-peg and thus more readily available. Rude girl fashion often consisted of tight knee-length skirts, often with zipper sides, sleeveless shirts, frequently in black and white, with dark red lipstick and shoulder length hair. This uniform made for an impressive collection at any ska gig where the archetypal ska dance, 'the skank', was performed.

As the second phase started to grip Britain in the late '70s, there was one new addition to the wardrobe - Dr. Martens. As ska and 2 Tone recruited increasingly large numbers of disenchanted punks, curious Mods and open-minded skinheads, the boot began to claim its stake in this new subculture. The greying of areas between skins and ska was accentuated by the popularity of the boots, especially when worn with Harrington jackets with red check linings, occasional braces, and button badges.

Also, some of the new revival Mods who picked up on ska first already wore DM's - Jerry Dammers himself wore many pseudo-Mod outfits, including a '60s single-breasted Mod suit bought in a second-hand shop, that provided the inspiration for a generation of 2 Tone fans. It was perhaps ironic that a man famous for his gap-toothed grin could become a fashion icon for thousands.

Furthermore, DM's seemed ideally suited to 2 Tone's clean cut, black and white image. The famous logo for the label was a character called Walt Jabsco (Walt after Walt Disney) - a man in a black suit, wearing black sunglasses, white shirt, black tie, pork pie hat, white socks and black loafers, next to the famous 2 Tone chequered pattern. This was a cartoon drawn by Dammers himself and based on Pete Tosh from the cover of a Wailing Wailers album. The shortened trousers also made the importance of the right footwear even more apparent, and even the soles of Docs were two tone. All of these factors quickly compounded to make the boots a staple item.

2 Tone as a label and a movement was relatively short-lived, with The Specials line-up splintering off into various solo projects, the label struggling through financial difficulties and Dammers himself being locked in legal wrangles for years. Like punk before it however, it had made an indelible mark on British culture.

Ska was originally a Jamaican dance music that emerged in the late '50s and prospered in the early '60s Kingston scene. Originally, it was derived from a mixture of traditional Jamaican mento, jazz, ya-ya and Calypso, as well as some north American influences. This melting pot of music was played at dance halls or on the back of huge lorries carrying massive, ear-splitting mobile sound systems. Ska historians point to Clement 'Sir Coxsone' Dodd (after the Yorkshire cricketer of the same name) as creating the first ska tracks in late 1960, just a few months after Dr. Martens first started making boots (although any connection between the two was still a long way off).

Ska was first imported to the UK via the West Indian immigrant population. On arrival here, it was also known as blue beat or Jamaican Blues, and from these early incarnations evolved first rocksteady and then reggae in the late '60s.

London enjoyed a particularly strong mid-to-late '60s ska scene. Many reggae stars started off playing ska, such as Bob Marley, Bunny Wailer and Peter Tosh, and they even sported cropped haircuts, a staple cut of working class subcultures. As more skinhead Jamaicans (known as 'Cocos pelados') moved to the UK, the style caught on, an evolution which makes a mockery of the later fascistic skinhead movements.

After some stage invasions got out of control and were exacerbated by racist violence at 2 Tone gigs, The London Evening News ran a piece on Selecter saying 'Don't rock with these Sieg Heilers.' This was despite the fact that only one of the seven band members was white, and that they were renowned for their anti-racist views and multi-cultural beliefs.

Allegedly, the first 2 Tone track was the eponymous single recorded by the Selecter in the garden shed of producer Roger Lomas.

In late '50s Jamaica, bassist Cluet Johnson played his brand of new music around town whilst greeting people with the phrase 'Love Skavoovie', from which the word 'ska' is seen by some to have been appropriated. Others claim it is derived from the sound of the hi-hat being opened and closed.

The name loafer comes from the German word 'LandLäufer' meaning "a wanderer, or vagabond."

In the post-punk, post-ska cauldron, Docs for once found few champions in British subculture. Soul and funk enjoyed an early '80s revival and the existentialist groups, who were clumsily dubbed 'the movement with no name', such as Echo and the Bunnymen did not really wear the boot.

Elsewhere, the New Romantic movement, with all its extravagance and embroidered finery also found little of interest in the simple uniform minimalism of the Doc Martens. The clique of disenchanted punk poseurs who led the New Romantic movement took their fascination with fashion to extreme levels. The Doc was rarely worn at New Romantic clubs like Louise's.

Also in 1980: Ronald Reagan (ex-actor) beats Jimmy Carter (ex-peanut farmer) into the White House; John Lennon assassinated; Post It notes launched; USA boycott Moscow Olympics; Who Shot JR? T shirts sell millions; Smallpox eradicated.

Buster

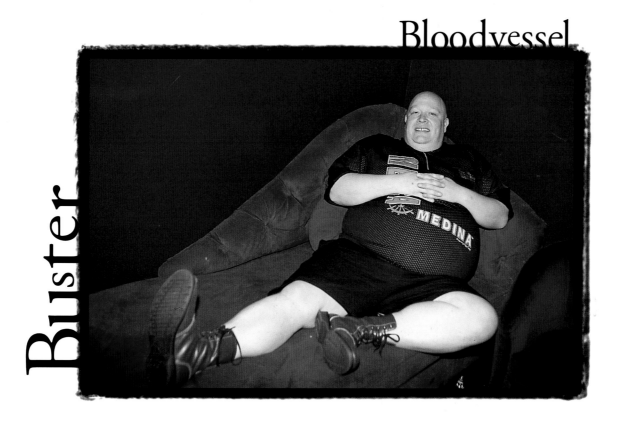

The inimitable Buster Bloodvessel, aka Doug Trendle, fronted another larger than life band - Bad Manners. Although many observers derided them for releasing novelty hits like 'Lip Up Fatty', 'Special Brew' and 'The Can Can' in the midst of 2 Tone's success, the band had actually been playing ska-influenced music since way back in 1975, under the name Stoop Solo and the Sheet Starchers. Bad Manners were actually offered a deal by 2 Tone but turned it down.

Buster's literally enormous presence (he weighs around 350 pounds) was an awesome live sight - aside from his frame, which was squeezed into large, dirty striped T-shirts, he has a thirteen inch tongue, is totally bald and apparently holds the world record for eating Big Macs - thirty in a row. His penchant for Dr. Martens boots is legendary. In one instance, he was flying back to Britain for a *Top of the Pops* performance, which he planned to do in full French can-can regalia. Unfortunately, import officers would not allow him to take his colossal bloomers through the customs, so on arrival at the BBC he had to rummage around their costume department for a suitable replacement. Then when he was about to go on stage, they refused to let him wear his beloved DM's. He said at the time, 'It was like cutting off my feet.'

Buster and Bad Manners were once on Epic America, the same label as Michael Jackson: "We couldn't figure out why they'd want a bunch of silly boys alongside him. It dawned on us later...we were a tax loss."

Also in 1981: Official announcement of a new killer virus, initially known as GRID but soon replaced by the monicker of AIDS; Prince Charles and Lady Diana Spencer marry; Pac Man video game introduced; Pope John Paul II shot; Space Shuttle makes debut launch; *MTV* launched.

MADNESS

Suggs

The Los Palmas Seven

One band who perhaps did more than any other to reinforce Dr. Martens in the hearts and minds of Britain's (and later America's) youth subculture was Madness. In 1974, they called themselves the Aldenham Glamour Boys, wore spray-painted Docs and imported Levi 501s, and drove ex-Post Office Morris Minor vans. When they came together as a band in 1976, they were initially called the North London Invaders, hailing as they did from the town of Camden. Evolving into Madness, the members were art student Mike Barson and two old schoolmates Chrissie Boy Foreman and Lee Thompson (who were at the time working together as gardeners), Graham 'Suggs' McPherson, Daniel Woodgate, Mark Bedford and later Cathal Smythe.

In the late '70s their ska influenced gigs garnered a small but loyal local following - although Suggs was once thrown out of the band for going to see a Chelsea football match instead of rehearsing! Then one night in the Hope & Anchor pub, they bumped into The Specials. Dammers and Suggs got talking, crude and basic demo tapes were handed over and support slots followed, including some superb shows at The Nashville, before Madness signed to 2 Tone for a one-off single, 'The Prince'.

This was the first of 21 Top 20 singles Madness released between 1979 and 1986, making them one of the greatest UK singles bands of all time. Signing in the longer term with Stiff Records, home to Ian Dury and the Blockheads, Madness set about producing a series of inspired, eclectic, often darkly humourous and always delightfully catchy records. First up was the single 'One Step Beyond' introduced by the now-legendary spoken words of seventh member Chas Smash

Finsbury Park, Madstock, 1998

(alias Cathal Smythe) "Hey You! Don't watch that, watch dis, this is the heavy, heavy monster sound..." The Nutty Sound had arrived. The album of the same name hit the No. 2 spot despite the later realisation that most of Thompson's saxophone was in fact in the wrong key! Around this time, Chas Smash, who until now had only been recruited for his dancing and on stage lunacy as Master of Ceremonies, was finally welcomed as a full-blown member.

Accompanying Madness' quite superb singles catalogue was a legion of unique promotional videos that made them a household name. Most famous was the clip used for the single 'Baggy Trousers', probably the greatest song ever written about schooldays. A constant factor in these mini-movies would be saxophonist Lee Thompson dangling from a wire over the heads of the rest of the band. The band's biggest commercial success, and amazingly their only No. 1 hit, May 1982's 'House of Fun', also had a similarly madcap video. In their long form videos, *Complete Madness* and *Utter Madness*, they even went to the legendary Holts shoe shop in Camden to buy some Docs. Other bands who had become regular visitors to the shop included The Specials and The Beat. The office above was also home to Trigger Management who looked after The Specials, and both bands would often watch *Top of the Pops* on the cheap television above the piles of Dr. Martens below.

MADNESS *the business*

Despite Madness' pop facade, they suffered problems with neo-fascists at their gigs - they probably had the biggest skinhead following of all the ska-related bands. Although Suggs had himself started off life as a skin, as indeed had Chas Smash, the band grew increasingly concerned about the political preferences of some of their crowd and the occasional outbreaks of violence. The single 'Embarrassment' was in fact about the ludicrous reaction of a racist to a mixed race child in his family.

Their final album, *Mad Not Mad*, which did not feature Barson, was chock-full of classic tracks and tragi-comic observations (Suggs was less keen - he said producing it had been like "polishing a turd"). Unfortunately, the album was recorded in an increasingly fractious atmosphere and in autumn 1986, Madness split up.

In the void left by the Camden Cowboys' absence however, their reputation grew. Scores of bands cited them as an influence and their back catalogue never stopped selling. Then, in 1992, the announcement was made that Madness were reforming for a one-off show at London's Finsbury Park, to be called 'Madstock'. The public's frenetic response was so strong that there have been several such reunions since.

In his last ever interview before his assassination, John Lennon said he admired Madness greatly.

The most globally recognisable influence of Madness has been the gratitude paid to them by America's so-called 'third wave of ska', namely bands such as No Doubt and the Mighty Mighty Bosstones.

A. H. Holts shoe shop once sold dozens of steel toe-capped DM's to a Japanese clothes designer, who then proceeded to cut the leather off the cap and sell them for £200 a pair.

The first pair of Doc. Martens I set foot in were Mad Pete McGhee's. I wanted a brand new pair (as you do when you are a 12 year old follower of fashion.) but, when I arrived at HOLTS in the Kentish Town Rd. I found that, because of my boot size (4) I could only purchase the "BABY DOC." With its lemon leather trim at the top & Stayprest Soul. No way was I forking out £3.10/-3d to look a half pint! So slightly peeved I took my weary Hob Nails up to Pete McGhee's. He dug me out a pair of one previous owner, 10 hole, full stitched soul un-punchured, Air Wair. So, on this sunny, Saturday in the summer of 69' the lads & myself, make our way to Madame Tusauds in the Marlebone Rd. The only hick-up being the size of Mr. McGhee's plates of! Although he was 14, he stood a good 5ft 8". So, we entered Tusauds in various positions. My size 8 or 9 D.M.S. (packed at the front of the boot with screwed up tabloid) way out in front of me, at the time thinking, "I look THE BOLLOCKS"!!! But in hind sight, "lost in a Waxworks . . . . All I needed was a red nose & to stand perfectly still.

HA, HA, HA, HA!

Pee Kip AKA Co-Co the Clown. X

HOLTS ceased trading on 19th Sept 1998. Alan you'll always be in my thoughts. LT

The '70s and start of the '80s saw Dr. Martens rule Britain's schoolyards. In some senses, 1979 was the year of the youth cult with a bizarre mix of parkas, punks, Mods, 2 Tone Rude boys, and even heavy metal denim jackets, inspired by the new wave of British heavy metal bands. Upgrading from your Monkey boots to your first pair of DM's was almost a cherished rite of passage. By contrast, the genuine terror felt when confronted by the school bully in his lofty 16 holers was felt by thousands of kids across Britain. Current AirWair Chairman, Stephen Griggs was quick-witted enough to box around this dilemma: "I wasn't a very tough boy but all the hard cases left me alone because I owed them pairs of DM's. They knew that if they beat me up I wouldn't deliver."

Tower of Strength

One of the longest lasting youth subcultures of all is goth. Spawned in the appropriately named Batcave club in London, 1981, the pale faced, black-clad, doom-obsessed bands quickly gathered a large and cult following, with a unique look that spread across many countries. Although *Alternative Press* magazine hailed Nico's 1969 album *The Marble Index* as the first goth album, many observers look towards the rise of Bauhaus or The Cramps, and other later bands like The Sisters of Mercy, The Cure, The Mission and Alien Sex Fiend.

Goth possesses a peculiar ability to stay out of the mainstream, which is perhaps why it has remained a subculture. Whilst punk was consumed and spat out by a headline-hungry media and copied by a hundred high street fashion stores, goth has stayed in the dark corners of its own making.

In America, many goth fans later picked up on the globally successful industrial music. This early '90s scene had many of the original elements of older goth - the fishnets, the black and white make-up for men and women, the jet black hair, although the music was much heavier. During 1994, industrial music was particularly popular, as a result of which millions of kids the world over donned black clothes and corresponding DM's.

Of course, certain characters transcend such genres and attain their own legendary status. Siouxsie Sioux has moved on from her days embroiled in London's punk scene to become an heroine for millions of goths worldwide. Since then she has formed the Creatures, along with Budgie, and has again reinforced her undoubted position as one of the unique subcultural icons of modern times.

When Robert Smith cut off his goth locks in 1986, MTV News broadcast updates every half hour for a day.

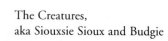

The Creatures,
aka Siouxsie Sioux and Budgie

Ich Bin Ein Auslander

"No true skinheads are racist. Without the Jamaican culture skinheads would not exist. It was their culture mixed with British working class culture that made Skinhead what it is."
Roddy Moreno of SHARP
(Skinheads Against Racial Prejudices)

The mutation of the original skinhead values into the tabloid scaring, violent beast that became the archetype, led to a counter-culture who fought to highlight this betrayal. Many had suffered at the hands of society or the police for their style, despite their liberal views - for example, skinhead folklore suggests that in one British town in the late '70s, anyone with a cropped haircut was not allowed to go out of their house after 10pm, under pain of arrest.

The '70s saw most problems with neo-Nazis and skinhead groups in the UK, whom non-racist skins often call 'boneheads.' Spearheading the musical branch of this anti-Nazi skinhead movement were the trio The Redskins. Once called No Swastikas, The Redskins united the left-wing skinhead movement with their brash, often belligerent and ranting punk hybrid. Lead singer Chris Dean, himself a writer for *NME*, renamed himself X. Moore - his lyrics were almost entirely political and gigs saw them berate fascists and right-wing politics ceaselessly. Indeed, they were all members of the Socialist Workers Party. Despite splitting up in 1986, the Redskins were just one strong example of the growing tide of anti-fascist feeling within the skinhead movement. Concerts by the Anti-Nazi League and Rock Against Racism have proved similarly potent in fighting this menace - for example, the 1978 Carnival Against the Nazis in Hyde Park was attended by over 80,000 kids who listened to The Clash, Tom Robinson Band and Steel Pulse. This event has been followed by scores of similar gigs over the years.

SHARP are just one of several skinheads organisations that fight prejudice and racism. In Germany in particular, there has been some very public fascist activity and even murders, which actually led to an increase in anti-fascist action. Of the estimated 8,000 skins in Germany, over 20% are believed to be converts of SHARP.

Inevitably, such close associations with skins have generated years of bad publicity for Dr. Martens. For a boot that was designed to alleviate pain, it is ironic that they first came to prominence for inflicting hurt. The toe cap, the thick sole, the supporting legs, all elements that make DM's so healthy, have been at times entirely hijacked by the more violent sections of society. Some observers called it 'a boxing glove for the feet' and tabloid pictures of old ladies with Dr. Martens prints on their faces did little to assuage public concern. Most likely, Klaus Maertens (who died in 1988) would have been horrified to see his medical invention used in such a fashion. At one point, AirWair were phoned up by one tabloid newspaper demanding to know why they continued to make boots that precipitated such violence. In response, Max Griggs said "It's not the boot that kicks heads in, it's the people who wear them. You can be violent in anything." Also, extreme right-wing groups tend to wear army boots with toe-caps, rather than DM's.

Regular revivals of skinheads have spread the culture to other countries - France, Germany, Australia, America, south America and after the collapse of Communism, Czechoslovakia and Hungary. All have large skinhead populations.

DM's laces have long had a colour code of their own. White laces on skins designated right-wing allegiance. Punks often preferred red laces, but these can also be worn to indicate left-wing tendencies. Lesbians often wear purple laces, as do goths. It is not known where or why these codes originated. Despite this, they were never universal, and people frequently had their own preferences that were devoid of any political or social connotations.

The boot has recently earned a very secure position in gay culture. Both lesbian women and gay men sport DM's of various styles, and they are often worn with some variant of the skinhead look, which has become fashionable in gay circles. The shoe is also popular, and on the fantastically colourful gay parades, the more extravagant Doc styles can also be seen.

Psychobilly

With the punk explosion giving England's youth the licence to rebel, the psychobilly phenomenon took up the baton gallantly. Flying in the face of classic rockabilly, it upset the purists with its anti-fashion stance. People crossed the road when a psychobilly approached - multi-coloured quiffs, bleached jeans, DM's half way up their legs and a multitude of tattoos prevailed. Rockabilly bands like The Stray Cats and Polecats had enjoyed chart success, whereas psychobilly was far less commercial, far more punk.

The first true psychobilly band was The Meteors, led by Paul P. Ferech. Often covered in fake blood, they were the pioneers of the movement and proclaimed "only The Meteors are pure psychobilly." The psychobilly mecca was the Klubfoot at the Clarendon in Hammersmith, west London.

The scene rapidly swept across Europe, Scandinavia and into Japan and for a few years it seemed every teenager on the underground had a quiff and tattoo. It was a club for rebels. London four piece, The Guana Batz, fronted by Pip Hancox, were a colossal live proposition and grabbed an army of demented followers. However, King Kurt were always the messiest! When word spread of their audiences throwing dead animals on stage along with tins of paint and bags of flour, venue bans quickly followed. Also riding high were Restless, Demented Are Go, Torment, Frenzy, Long Tall Texans, The Milkshakes and The Sting Rays with the cabaret provided by the Highliners.

The music industry hated psychobilly - which just made it even more fun.

The Meteors and crew

Also in 1982: First liposuction performed.; Acid rain recognised.; Madonna's first single released; Falklands War breaks out; *ET* becomes the biggest grossing film of all time; Michael Jackson's *Thriller* album becomes the biggest selling album of all time.

Also in 1983: The Green Party rise to prominence in Germany but many people scoff at their environmental concerns; *The Thorn Birds* rules TV sets the world over; Apple introduce the computer mouse; Camcorders for sale in shops; Vinyl lovers the world over laugh at the latest fad — compact disc; Crack cocaine surfaces on the streets of America.

Snakebite and Klubfoot

"Tonight we are armpit deep in broken glass, solidifying sweat and brain-dead soulless psychobillies with tattoos on their foreheads and bloodlust in their eyes all hunting for live brains to nourish their rotting flesh as every horror in London assembles. Things quickly get out of hand as huge evil mutant flat top monsters take over the dance floor to wrench and claw at each other in the terrifyingly violent ritual of rockabilly dancing. I try fighting my way down the front but I'm beaten back by a hideously malevolent deathwalker messily devouring a weaker victim."

'Back, you evil spawn of hell,' I scream, 'You are blocking my view of the lead guitarist.' I clutch my crucifix but against these creatures it is of little use. A few, the dim light of proto-intelligence shining feebly in their eyes, battle with equally foul bouncers and intestines fly in the ensuing carnage as more zombies pile on top, naked flesh gleaming with raw blood and splattered human remains. I am backed into a corner and resolve to sell my life dearly. Four of the creatures start eating my girlfriend.

'Don't kill her,' I protest, 'She is paying my bus fare home.'

Mercifully the gig ends and the walking dead shuffle off, shoulders hunched, flesh dribbling from mouths. I find I am limping. One of my feet has been bitten off. Never mind, it's a small price to pay. The Guana Batz were fab."

Review of a Guana Batz gig at the London Clarendon Klubfoot by fiction author Martin Millar in the NME.

Smeg of King Kurt

Early Guana Batz, songwriter Stuart Osbourne

Psychobillies

King Kurt's live chaos

Pip of the Guana Batz

Love
and
Pride

Paul King

In 1985, British meteorologists first confirmed that there was a gaping hole in the ozone over the Antarctic, Rock Hudson became Hollywood's first big name casualty to die of Aids, Greenpeace's Rainbow Warrior was bombed by French agents and the Rock 'n' Roll Hall of Fame was inaugurated. Mainstream music offered us Whitney Houston's debut album and Dire Straits *Brothers In Arms*. Back in Coventry, half a decade after 2 Tone, one band was surfacing that would change the face of Dr. Martens boots forever.

King, the brainchild of lead singer Paul King, hit the No. 2 spot in early 1985 with their single 'Love And Pride'. Paul King had been a twelve year old suedehead fascinated by Bowie, glam and then 2 Tone. After his previous band, The Reluctant Stereotypes, split up, he formed King, who struggled with their first three singles (including one called 'Sole On My Boot') before 'Love And Pride' broke through. Their manager, Perry Haines, went on to found and edit the seminal fashion publication *i-D* magazine.

King's fashion sense was a unique mixture of skinhead and glam. Wearing short trousers, long quiffed hair and large boots, King himself called the unique hybrid a "psychedelic skin look" or "multi-tone" rather than 2 Tone. He was fascinated by the *Clockwork Orange* look, and was heavily influenced by Bowie, whose own Ziggy Stardust project had also been highly affected by that film. The band's chief trademark, however, were their multi-coloured Dr. Martens. Each television performance saw them appear with different coloured boots on their feet - indeed, the 'Love And Pride' video saw the band and dozens of kids spraying their boots multi-colours on screen. King's Docs were also often decorated with straps across the laces, buckles, patent leather and in one instance, hand-painted with a portrait of the singer.

The boots became such a feature of the band's success that AirWair approached King, who were subsequently given various pairs, including one with flashing lights on the sole. British teen magazine *Smash Hits* reflected Paul King's heart-throb status by running a feature headlined 'How To Paint Your DM's Like King', and style bible *The Face* also featured their music and footwear. When the band appeared on *Top of the Pops*, King wore a custom-made gold pair.

One evening on tour, Paul King met J.J. Burnel of the Stranglers, famous for his all black look and black 1460s. They spotted each other in the bar, Burnel approached King and said "So, you're the one who wears those multi-coloured DM's - I think they should always be black myself."

Paul King himself had seen coloured Docs way back in 1974. "I first saw them at football matches. When Coventry played Chelsea at football, the London skins were into Bowie and called themselves Bowie Bootboys. They wore big DM's painted in Chelsea blue."

In many ways, King's championing of the boot was the first public time that they had been associated with an entirely non-violent movement - when added to his sex appeal, this meant that the boots were exposed to a whole new generation (and gender) of wearers.

This was only spotted after AirWair noted a large increase in the sale of boys sizes, later realising this was actually girls purchasing the smaller boot. King abruptly disbanded in 1986 after two excellent but under-rated albums.

Also in 1986: Chernobyl nuclear reactor melts down; Challenger Shuttle explodes seconds after lift-off; Imelda Marcos abandoned state home in the Philipines reveals her collection of 1060 pairs of shoes, but no DM's.

The Cure

The Cure formed back in 1978, and although several of the key band members did not actually wear DM's - many preferred pointed suede boots or in Robert Smith's case, oversized tongues on white basketball boots - Simon Gallup frequently wore knee-high Docs.

"Dr. Martens? I hate them."

Shane MacGowan

The Pogues name is taken from the Gaelic expression 'pogue mahone', meaning 'kiss my ass.'

Alan Wilder during his time in Depeche Mode

"I may no longer be in DM, but I still like DM's."

View from the stage, Jo Boxers

A rash of British bands in the mid-80s wore Doc Martens. Arguably the finest band of that period, The Smiths, saw lead singer Morrissey frequently wearing both the shoe and the boot. His followers wore similar clothes and mimicked his trademark quiff almost religiously. This, along with King, was another early example of girls wearing DM's for perhaps the first time. The Smiths generated a cult following that has rarely been equalled in British music, and their slew of brilliant singles rejuvenated a rather tired and unimaginative British music scene. Since his solo career started, Morrissey has enjoyed more global success than the Smiths ever achieved.

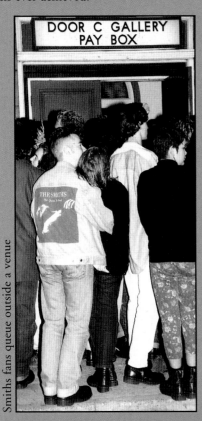

Smiths fans queue outside a venue

"As precocious teenagers we rebelled against the staid Teddy Boy image and fashion of crepe shoes and drape suits by wearing regulation council issue donkey jackets, lumberjack shirts, turned up Levis and DM's, sometimes with steel toe-caps (sometimes exposed), which would also come in handy during the odd scrap with Neasden skins. Then later, during the early Polecats shows, we used to jump around like epileptic grasshoppers and DM's were the only shoe to grip well on any stage surface, covered with any amount of beer and bodily fluids."

Boz, latterly Morrissey's guitarist and collaborator.

Morrissey

Rat of Ned's Atomic Dustbin

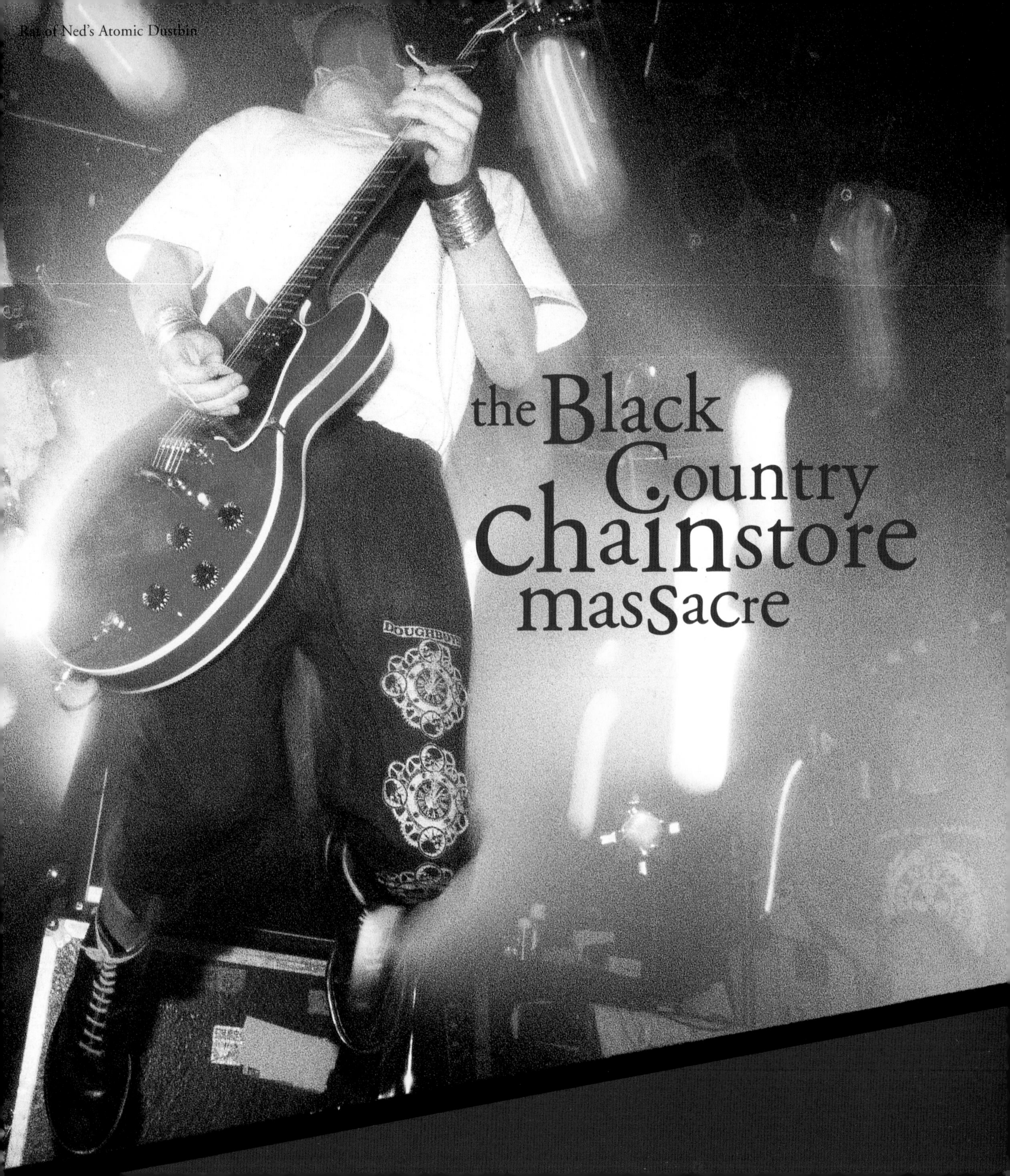

the Black Country Chainstore massacre

Grebo girls
camp down for the night

Carter USM

In the late '80s and early '90s, a rash of bands from the Midlands town of Stourbridge burst on to the music scene, and were quickly dubbed 'grebo', a word taken from a Pop Will Eat Itself track. Ned's Atomic Dustbin and the Wonder Stuff were the other two key players, along with bands such as Carter the Unstoppable Sex Machine and Mega City Four. Although all of these bands were sonically diverse, the loosely-based movement, and its thousands fans, dominated the British alternative music scene for two years. The standard choice of footwear was almost exclusively Dr. Martens, with the accompanying loud, sloganeering band T-shirts selling in their thousands.

> "These children that you tastefully spit on have, for months, been spreading like mould on muck."
>
> Billy Batty in *The Face*.

"DM's are the perfect lived in footwear, an extended part of your soul really. I wore my oldest pair to Reading festival in 1997 and they were covered in mud. I thought to myself 'This is where we have to split up, finally, after all these years.' So when I got back to my hotel room, I held a small funeral service and took some polaroids of the boots, before I carefully placed them in the bin. It was like putting down a pet."

Steve Lamacq, BBC Radio 1 *Evening Session* DJ.

Teetering like Bambi on acid

"Don't let your vanity be imposed upon by those persuasive articles on wearing pin-point heels for shopping in the morning...the number of males on the loose during shopping hours is narrowly limited."

Extract from *The Intelligent Woman's Guide to Good Taste*, 1958

Things have changed somewhat since the launch of the first Dr. Martens boot. Although women have been wearing DM's for years, this was generally by punks or skins, and they preferred the 1460 or the shoe, but only if they could find a size small enough. However, in the mid-80s, everything changed.

The fashions of that decade found women dressing for themselves, not for men, and the mélange of styles and ideas saw seemingly inappropriate items being thrown together in new combinations. It was thus that the classic style of a flowery dress with a big pair of clumpy Docs found its way into many girls' wardrobes. The boots tempered the overt femininity of the pretty dresses, and at the same time reduced any inherent vulnerability that such flimsy garments might portray. Sociologists hailed the new trend as an emancipation of sorts, whilst many ardent feminists championed the boot and shoe as a symbol of their assertiveness. Such 'proletarian chic', as some observers called it, was a distinct rebellion against more traditional women's clothing.

For other girls, it was just a great relief to be wearing a comfortable pair of shoes. Throughout history, women's footwear has been far from practical. Chinese foot-binding was an extreme example that had been used to manacle women under the control of men centuries ago. In 17th century Europe, male spouses insisted that their women wear heeled shoes, making it virtually impossible for these ladies to walk on the cobbled streets outside. Indeed, when the flat-soled, weather-proof boot was introduced for women in the 1830s, there was outrage amongst the less liberal men of society, horrified by the newly mobile women. Over in France, one of the charges against Joan of Arc was that "she dressed in men's boots up her thighs."

For the modern woman, the stiletto was similarly debilitating. Apart from the sexual connotations, the shoe was never ideally suited to lengthy walking, nor offered any degree of security in the event of a difficult situation.

Many feminists saw the stiletto as a natural descendant of Chinese foot-binding. By contrast, Docs accentuated the foot and looked strong and well-constructed, in turn purveying an impression of power and independence.

The burgeoning women's market led to a flurry of fantastic Dr. Martens styles, colours and patterns, many initially based around a variant of the 1460. Such extravagance was not new however - in the 1890s, opera boots were hand-painted with detailed flowers and proved very popular in English high society. The rising demand for girls' DM's eventually led to more innovative styles such as high-heeled DM's, which were introduced in autumn 1993, and even platform soles, called Quads. Designers hooked on to the idea, anchoring the frail look of many of their catwalk creations with a solid pair of Docs.

The most entertaining aspect of this development was the absolute horror and consternation created by girls wearing Docs. Vast sections of society seemed to lose faith in human nature, and hastily predicted the downfall of Generation X. Parents were appalled to see their beautiful daughter wearing the same boots as a skinhead. The media had many doubters - take this extract from a clearly unimpressed Mike Lockley of *The Rugeley Post*, 'Do today's young women honestly believe Doc Martens boots go with dresses? Or they look more alluring with studs in their noses?'

All this disapproval mattered little - by 1994, 50% of Dr. Martens-wearers were women. It is quite ironic that the workwear boot that first came to notoriety for its macho image is now regarded by many as the quintessential unisex footwear. It is fair to say that Doc Martens have revolutionised shoe fashion for women - a sixteen year old girl is now far more likely to buy a pair of DM's as her first solo purchase than a traditional women's shoe or a teetering pair of stilettos.

In the same summer as the DM's original launch, Dr. W. Bamber wrote in *Shoe & Leather News* that society should "Ban all stiletto heels - how women can balance in them I don't know...the answer is to encourage girls to wear sensible shoes, but I am afraid the dictates of fashion might prevail."

"Women have been ingratiating themselves to men for too long. If you want to be nice to men, then there are plenty of ways of doing so that don't involve wearing ridiculous shoes on your feet."

Dr. Halla Beloff, a Social psychologist at Edinburgh University.

Blessed Ethel

"Women's shoes helped to enforce the vision of the ideal woman as a weak and sedentary creature who lives almost entirely indoors."

A shoe historian.

"Just look at the way women walk in a pair of Doc Martens or whatever. Bold, confident and mobile. No more teetering about like Bambi on acid..."

Jane Owen, extract from her novel, *Camden Girls*.

The high heeled DM's boot was tested by Stephen Griggs' own postmistress, Mary Barnes.

"Everyone's

Peter Stringfellow, King of Clubs

an individual."

From these Muddy Pastures...

Many people see the Monterey Pop Festival as the first of the great rock festivals - descended from the Monterey Jazz and Folk Festival, this 1967 event saw a spectacularly destructive performance by The Who and Jimi Hendrix's infamous guitar-burning during his extraordinary rendition of 'Wild Thing'. Since then a crop of festivals have evolved - Woodstock, Live Aid, Glastonbury, Reading and Lollapalooza to name but a few.

British festivals are lead by the Glastonbury weekend, attended most years by tens of thousands, fully prepared to face the usual onslaught of mud baths and long toilet queues. Despite this, the weekend has a cherished place in most British festival-goers hearts. Its enigmatic organiser, farmer Michael Eavis (a loyal DM's wearer) revealed how this legendary festival started off in bizarre circumstances: "The first problem was that I knew nothing about the music business. I started by ringing up Colston Hall in Bristol to ask how I could get in touch with pop groups. A chap there gave me the name of an agent, and the agent put me in touch with the Kinks, who agreed to appear for £500, which was a lot of money for me to pull out of a milk churn...I was ready to give up. I woke up every morning before milking time worrying about how much it was costing me, thinking it was doomed to failure..."

At that first Glastonbury festival in September 1970, Eavis handed out free milk and provided a large ox roast (which was hijacked by hungry Hells Angels). Also, despite local pubs posting signs saying 'Hippies Keep Out', there was a strong turn-out. Unfortunately, Eavis still managed to lose £1500. However, through its more hippyfied days of the '70s and massive headline slots by enormous global acts such as Prodigy, Pulp, Radiohead and New Order, Glastonbury has become established as perhaps the definitive UK festival.

The famous loved-up Woodstock festival of August 1969 was intended to be a highly organised and commercially-minded event. Originally, there were 186,000 tickets sold, with police expecting around 200,000 people to attend at most. However, on the weekend in question, over one million turned up at Max Yasgur's farm in Bethel, New York. Within hours, the $18 entrance fee was abandoned and the event turned into a free festival, as security could do little to keep the swarming masses out. As the most chronicled example of its genre, these 'Three Days of Peace And Music', saw three deaths, two births and four miscarriages.

As the years went by, festivals mutated into a more potent creature. Instead of being a gathering for gathering's sake, the mass events were turned to political or social ends. Anti-racism, gay liberation, animal rights, the homeless and scores of charitable and other issues have benefited from festival income over the years. The biggest profile fund-raiser of them all was, of course, 1985's Live Aid. Inspired by Bob Geldof, lead singer of the Boomtown Rats, who was moved to act by a shocking BBC documentary about the Ethiopian famine, the event followed on from his collaborative Christmas single, 'Do They Know It's Christmas?' which featured a host of British names and became the best-selling UK single of all time.

The earliest **footwear** was made from plaited **grass**,
held together with **thongs**, and provided protection for the wearer

when **walking** across rough **terrain** in inclement **weather**.

By the close of the day, with a simultaneous event in Philadelphia's JFK Stadium, and watched by a global audience of over 1.8 billion people, Geldof and his colleagues had started a phenomenon that would go on to generate over $50 million.

In recent times, the most potent festival has been the eclectic collection of bands and issues on view at Lollapalooza. This travelling festival was the brainchild of Perry Farrell, of Jane's Addiction and Porno For Pyros. The debut touring package showcased a myriad of musical styles whilst offering information about a variety of important issues, thus creating an environment and forum for debate. At each stadium-sized show there would be stalls organised by major and minor protest groups, such as Greenpeace, gun control lobbyists and civil liberties groups. Tattooists and fire-eaters added to the general Bohemian atmosphere and the resultant tour package was a phenomenal success - in many senses this was in fact the real Woodstock 2 (the actual Woodstock 2, in 1994, was generally viewed as disappointing). The list of bands who have played Lollapalooza is awesome including Ice T, Red Hot Chili Peppers, Henry Rollins and Ministry. Despite the recession at the time, the festival proved to be an outstanding success and has been repeated several times since. More recently, the Beastie Boys Tibetan Freedom concerts have also captured the youth's imagination, despite being struck by lightning during the 1998 show.

Due to the frequent mud-baths that festivals create, Docs have become a staple item of any festival-goers bag for the weekend. In the late '80s in the UK, when the so-called grebo scene was dominating the alternative, Reading was awash with both mud and 1460s. Similarly in 1992, when Nirvana played the same festival, amid backstage rumours that Kurt Cobain was using heroin again, a generation of grunge kids paraded their eight holers in similar quantities. As the thousands of kids trudged home, with their boots spattered in mud and their hands full of flyers, they did not know that this was the last time Kurt Cobain and Nirvana would ever perform in England.

"I regarded the whole thing as a cross between a harvest festival and a pop festival."

Michael Eavis

A Time to Travel

The British traveller is generally regarded to have begun life around the time of the 1974 Stonehenge People's Free Festival, which itself was a descendent of the Isle of Wight festivals of the previous decade. In 1970, the Windsor Free Festival was covered in the squatters slogan 'Pay no rent' and other events around this time were filled with like-minded individuals.

Key figures such as Sid Rawles, Bill Ubique Dwyer, Dr. John and Wally Hope were instrumental in creating the free festival movement, often inspired by slogans imported from America's west coast, a legacy of the Haight-Asbury days. This loved-up vibe evolved in the '70s into a more pro-active political slant. Travellers looked back to English groups of the 1600s and writers like Gerrard Winstanley of the Diggers, who tried to reclaim common land for the oppressed.

Many travelling festival-goers soon progressed to an entire lifestyle on the road, creating mini-mobile societies as they roved around the country. Inevitably, this led to clashes with society and the establishment. One such flashpoint is Stonehenge, the prehistoric monument which saw its first Solstice festival in 1974, instigated by Wally Hope. His group squatted at the site for most of that year. Now, it is closed to public access constantly, a decision that has evoked many angry protests and clashes with police. Many travelling communities have been the subject of both hysterical media coverage and oppressive government legislation (in particular the recent Criminal Justice Bill) in recent times, despite the fact that most are almost entirely pacific and self-sufficient, with education, work, recreation and social facilities of their own. Nevertheless, publications like *The Daily Telegraph* still deem it necessary to call them "a swarming tribe of human locusts."

At the 1975 Windsor Free festival, seven picnickers, five on-lookers, nine journalists and four welfare organisations were watched over by 350 riot police.

"When the earth has been **ravaged** and the animals are dying, a **tribe** of people from all races and all **creeds** shall put their faith in deeds not words. They shall be known as **Warriors** of the **rainbow**, protectors of the environment."

Hopi Indian Prophecy

A brief glossary of travellers' terms:

Blat - a short journey, usually for pleasure.

Diddish - something associated with traditional travellers, possibly degrading.

Geodesic Dome - a prefabricated structure of metal bars forming a grid of polygons, over which plastic or tarpaulin is stretched.

Fascists - the police.

Orbital - person who lives permanently in the vicinity of one settlement.

Feds - the police.

Old Bill - the police.

Pigs - the police.

Silly season - police reference to summer festivals.

Straight - house dweller.

Tatting down - clearing all possessions away prior to moving on.

Filth - the police.

"The portable alternative to flushing the loo is hygienic, safe, convenient, ecologically sound, multi-functional, and user-friendly - get a spade - bury your shit!"
Traveller poster

"Doc Martens boots have become phenomenally popular throughout the teenage population (reflecting) the basic traveller's wardrobe."
Extract from *A Time To Travel* by Fiona Earle et al.

"Willis Elf is wearing a pair of Doc Martens which have been painted and decorated with a constellation of silver stars. These stars are already disappearing behind a nebula of mud. Such is the detrimental effect of being in this place that I am now capable of holding a conversation with a man who calls himself Willis Elf and paints stars on his boots, and not minding too much. A very poor state for me to be in."

Martin Millar, extract from his novel
Love and Peace with Melody Paradise

Mark Chadwick and Rev Hammer of The Levellers talk to Tony Benn MP

Mark Chadwick of The Levellers

One band who have been regularly associated with travellers is The Levellers. Formed in Brighton, Sussex, their mix of folk instrumentation and rock and punk ethics proved a popular melting pot of ideas. "We draw on some Celtic influences because it's a powerful source, but we're a very English band." Their name and ideology was inspired by the socio-political activity at the time of the English Civil War in the mid-1600s. Their *Levelling The Land* album in 1991 was a huge commercial success in the UK, backed by an enigmatic live following that was famed for its unswerving loyalty.

One subculture that Doc Martens enjoyed little popularity in was the British rave scene. Although occasionally seen on the feet of dancing kids, the boots were not the footwear of choice (trainers tended to rule the day). However, the illicit nature of these massive raves, the cutting edge music, the pirate radio transmissions and establishment disapproval meant that many people who were soon caught up in the scene came from other subcultures and did indeed wear DM's.

Scene from the Poll Tax riots, Trafalgar Square, London 1990, described by Prime Minister Margaret Thatcher as "a little local difficulty."

"During the riots **the soles** sometimes melted if you got **too** near a **petrol** bomb."

"The film crew and I were travelling in a BBC armoured car on our way back to the airport when we came under attack. [Adie was hit in the foot] At the time I didn't think too much about it. I knew we'd sustained a hit on the vehicle but to be honest there wasn't a scratch on the boot, though I could feel my foot bleeding inside. When we examined the boot closely we found a tiny cut in the leather and two lumps in my foot...two bits of metal pierced the leather at such speed that the leather had actually closed back over the entrance points. There is still a bit of bullet in my foot. I bought those boots some time ago when I was sent to cover the Gulf War."

Kate Adie in Bosnia.

THE POLICE DO A GOOD
JOB PROTECTING PEOPLE
THEY ARE GOD'S SERVANTS,
THEY SHOULD BE ARMED
WITH SUB-MACHINE GUNS
TO PROTECT THEM
FROM EVIL DOERS
GOD BLESS THE GOOD
POLICE WROTE BY
JOHN !!!

"Take only pictures, leave only footprints, kill only time

A road protester defies the authorities

10% of one **homeless** charity's

86% of **young** homeless people are **forced** to **leave** home

25% of single **homeless** people are under **25** years old

hostel **occupants** were University educated

Dollars and HaVoc

Prior to the 1990s, Seattle was not famed for its alternative music. Of course, it could claim Jimi Hendrix amongst its forefathers, and there were other successes such as the Sonics, the Fleetwoods, and several more mainstream artists such as Robert Cray, Heart, Kenny G, Quincy Jones and Queensryche. However, these successes were sporadic and isolated, with no thread of association between the respective artists.

However, as the '80s headed towards a climax, an underground scene was developing that would, during a brief flurry of breath-taking musical brilliance, turn the global mainstream on its head. Grunge.

Starting in that cold, northwestern corner of the United States, grunge began life as a disparate group of bands gigging relentlessly on the underground circuit, with no real eye for the ensuing avalanche of multi-platinum record sales and sold-out world tours. The record label *Sub Pop* is seen by many as at the very nucleus of this era of music, releasing a seminal series of limited edition records, in the process airing classic tracks by bands such as Sonic Youth, Steve Fisk, the U-Men, Skinny Puppy, Nirvana, and the often overlooked Green River.

Aside from these names, there were hordes of other bands producing alternative music of note in this period. The quite brilliant Tad, Mudhoney, the Screaming Trees - these and many others released music that, to the youth of the day at least, was revolutionary. Older bands like the Melvins and Sonic Youth also enjoyed rejuvenated careers in the wake of numerous citations from the younger bands they had influenced. Older detractors derided grunge's fusion of hardcore and metal as merely re-hashing '70s rock, but this mattered little to those who were experiencing such music for the first time. It felt like they were living through something *important*. Besides, the scuzzy, furious raw energy of grunge was rooted much more in the post-punk barrage of US hardcore bands like Black Flag (who were themselves compared to bands like Led Zeppelin). Also, there was a clear lineage back to '60s garage bands like the Sonics, MC5, the Stooges and the Kingsmen.

Tad Doyle and Kurt Danielson

Like all subcultures and musical movements, this latest development was only tagged after it had already been around for some time (indeed, the term grunge itself was originally a tongue-in-cheek name). By then Nirvana had gone global with their ten million-selling *Nevermind* album, which single-handedly changed the face of modern music programming, live shows, record store buying policies and just about every facet of the music and entertainment industries. For example, in the wake of 'Smells Like Teen Spirit', *MTV*'s aesthetic was virtually transformed overnight, ditching the bikini-clad babes of a thousand soft porn metal videos and replacing them with grunge's more gritty, cheaper look. For the next two years, grunge ruled the world.

With the music came the culture - grunge, like punk before it, was truly thrift store chic. Bedecked in flannel shirts, oversized shorts cut off just below the knee and long, lank hair, the grunge kid quickly picked up the tag of 'loser'. Girls often wore flowery dresses with thick

Unfortunately, as with so many subcultures, once grunge entered the mainstream it was effectively rendered culturally impotent by its own success. Nirvana's debut album was produced for just $606.17 - now, cheque book-waving A&R men were jetting into Seattle and throwing six figure sums at almost any band. Some of these gambles paid off with multi-million selling albums, but many bands never achieved what they promised, unprepared as they were for the intense heat of the worldwide spotlight.

Million dollar marketing campaigns backed all the latest 'grungers', whilst cheesy TV shows ran features on what to say to your 'loser' teenager. Elevator music albums were released with muzak versions of grunge classics, and perhaps worst of all, haute couture designers started to copy the style. Milan and Paris catwalks exhibited horrendous copies of the grunge look, with obscenely priced and hideously shaped versions of the thrift store style. Record stores reported fashion journalists, dripping

"Grunge is what happens when children of divorce get their hands on guitars."

Newsweek.

leggings, or trousers with oversized band T-shirts. And on the feet of both the male and female grunge kids were invariably a pair of DM's, usually black, more often than not the 1460 (despite the recent rash of more flamboyant designs). Laces were frequently coloured and left untied, so that the sides of the quarter flapped loosely around the ankles. Band logos were occasionally painted on the boot, although generally the look was very simple and unfettered by decoration. This was dressing down at its ultimate extreme - the boot's status as an anti-label fitted perfectly with the anti-establishment feeling.

After the nadir of the late-80s, when Dr. Martens sales plummeted, this adoption by grunge re-opened the floodgates for Docs, sending the boot, for the first time, in vast quantities into Australasia, the USA, Japan and many other territories. After a lengthy phase when trainers had ruled the footwear world, it was a welcome return.

in designer garments, running in and asking for albums by grunge bands. Some even tried to re-title the designer wear 'frunge'. Lumberjack shirts with designers names were selling for over $500 and a corduroy jacket, similar to the thousands of second-hand coats worn by grunge fans, was offered for sale for $3000.

And then of course, it all stopped. The shot that was heard across the world, when Kurt Cobain committed suicide in early April 1994, effectively put an end to grunge, although for many it had already become listless amidst the corporate hijack, the growing drug problems and the increasingly feeble music. In the vacuum left by Cobain's death, the grunge movement splintered and stumbled. Fortunately, in America, bands like Green Day and Offspring filled the void with their post-punk energy, and were met with multi-million sales, as there still seemed to be a thirst for the punk ethos.

Also in the early '90s: Political correctness; MacDonalds opens restaurant in Moscow; Gulf War erupts.

Foo Fighters

Dr. Martens infiltration into the United States can actually be traced back much earlier than grunge. The Californian punk and hardcore scene at the start of the '80s found a home for the hard-to-find boot almost a decade before its west coast companion. Predominantly based in Los Angeles and San Francisco, bands like the Crowd, China White, Black Flag the Adolescents, the Outsiders and Social Distortion played hard-edged alternative music with a strictly underground feel. Amongst the masses at many of these sweaty gigs could be found dozens of pairs of DM's, despite the fact that only a handful of specialist stores stocked the imported boot at this early stage.

Interestingly, in light of future developoments, as many girls wore the boots in the scene as did men. However, these early converts experienced the same problem as that endured by skinhead girls - getting hold of smaller sizes. In the mid-80s, Docs were especially popular with girls on this scene, although brothel creepers and Monkey boots were also worn.

America also had its own skinhead scene which championed the boot a little later on, after which a series of subcultures found a place for it. Rockabilly and psychobillies, ska, industrial music and several other underground scenes have since fostered the boot as almost standard issue.

"All the best bands are tribes."
Henry Rollins 1995

Depeche Mode

There are few bands who have been so complex, vital, innovative and successful as Depeche Mode. This Essex band, formed out of schoolboy friendships and a love for alternative music, have produced album after album of quite inspirational music. Their take on the industrial scene, their own groundbreaking use of technology, and their simply breath-taking live shows have taken stadium music on to a new level. Mammoth tours, taking in all corners of the globe, have transformed them over the years from a relatively lightweight British pop band into a multi-faceted, multi-layered rock behemoth. In addition, their presentation has always been impeccable, with their instantly identifiable videos and art photography mostly being taken by the legendary photographer Anton Corbijn.

Their on-tour difficulties and Dave Gahan's much-publicised battles with health problems have often been overly-emphasised by the media, but this should not be allowed to mask the fact that they are both one of the biggest bands of all time, as well as one of the most creative. At the epicentre of this unique creativity is the songwriting genius of Martin Gore.

Martin Gore by Anton Corbijn

Snarled Up in the Suburbs

The last great British musical era of the '80s was in the spring of 1989, with the so-called Madchester scene - the Mancunian corner of the music world once again provided a plethora of bands revolutionising the rock and dance format - The Stone Roses led the way with The Happy Mondays and Inspiral Carpets following closely behind, as 'baggy' music swept the nation up in a tide of flares, long sleeved shirts and Joe Bloggs clothing. There was no place in this fashion for eight hole boots, only brand name trainers. Also, these bands struggled to export their culture across the Atlantic to America, a problem that many British groups of the next ten years endured, as the States found little of interest in the various English genres that sprang up.

This was certainly the case for the next upsurge of British talent - Britpop. The first whiffs of this new movement came in 1993 with the early singles of a band called Suede, led by the enigmatic and inspirational Brett Anderson. Set against a back-drop of slacker-driven grunge culture, whereby American music and fashion had dominated the British alternative scene since 1991, Suede's songs talked of highly stylised, romantic London dramas, and Brett's peculiar camp Englishness carried it all off to perfection. Suede had swagger, style and above all the songs - they were heralded by *Melody Maker* with an infamous front page headline reading 'The Best New Band In Britain.' They did indeed change the face of British music - it was a million miles from grunge's by-now tiring machismo and mainstream corporate feel.

The explosion of Britpop was pre-empted by a clumsily titled scene called the New Wave of New Wave, Doc Martens or trainer-wearing, speed-snorting energetic bands who were as important sartorially as they were musically - SMASH, Elastica and These Animal Men worshipped bands like The Clash and the Sex Pistols, but enjoyed only fleeting success as the approaching juggernaut of Britpop pushed them aside.

Britpop really started to blossom in 1993, boosted by Blur's pivotal second album, *Modern Life Is Rubbish*, which openly paraded their Anglo-centric interests. With the fading recession and the sense of gloom that had made grunge seem so appropriate in the UK, the kids began to look for something more uplifting. The much-anticipated arrival of Suede's eponymous debut album signalled another step away from the spiralling self-destructive tendencies of grunge-by-numbers. The festivals that bands like Nirvana and Pearl Jam had revitalised were now taken over by a string of newly confident British bands - Blur, Suede, The Boo Radleys, Pulp, and even a rejuvenated New Order.

The untimely death of Kurt Cobain and the arrival of Blur's third album *Parklife* sparked the deluge. Suddenly, there was a wash of superb British bands, with quirky albums and massive followings. British youth abruptly put their grunge clothing away and started rifling through their British bands' records again. Cut-off shorts and plaid shirts were returned to the charity stores, and long hair was cut short. In came a variant of the early '80s casual look, mixed with elements of Mod and other unique styles, including the odd Hawaiian shirt! Trainers were popular, Harrington jackets made another comeback and even the Oxfam look of Pulp's Jarvis Cocker was copied by many Britpop fans.

Once again, Dr. Martens managed to be accepted by this new generation of music. Many of the Britpop bands had listened to the likes of The Clash, Buzzcocks, Madness, 2 Tone and other Doc-saturated subcultures as kids, and now they were in a band themselves, they emulated their own heroes, and were in turn aped by their own generation of followers. This self-perpetuating cycle of influence has effectively kept Doc Martens at the heart of subculture virtually since the boot's inception.

In the next splendid eighteen months, Pulp finally broke their fourteen year duck and produced a sexually subversive, comical seedy masterpiece in their first major label album *His 'n' Hers*. Elastica, the Auteurs and the soon-to-be global Radiohead also all made an impact. Supergrass' debut album *I Should Coco* hit No. 1 and

Noel Gallagher of Oasis suffered from a kidney infection as a child and was allowed to wear long trousers to school,

"I wore Doc Martens as well and looked dead cool."

a litany of other bands enjoyed purple patches as well, including Shed Seven, Portishead, The Bluetones, Marion and Dodgy.

The Mod movement also enjoyed an indirect boost and mini-revival as well, with the so-called Modfather, Paul Weller, enjoying some of his biggest successes to date. Elsewhere, live music experienced a resurgence, band merchandise sales rocketed, festivals were repeatedly sold out and record shops couldn't stock enough of Britpop acts.

Unfortunately, the international appeal of these bands was limited. Oasis, the late-comers who took all the honours, obviously enjoyed great worldwide success, but they tended to wear the brown shoe and were rarely seen in Docs. This was also the case for one of their support bands who came good, The Verve. Generally America found the ironic and quirky Britpop scene rather unappealing.

Back in Britain, Britpop couldn't last of course. By the time Blur and Oasis were engaging in their féted battle for the No. 1 slot in August 1995, there were already dissenters who bemoaned the mainstream prostitution of the scene, just like glam, punk, grunge and many others before it. By mid-1996, with most of the big Britpop players recording new material and on sabbaticals, the movement was effectively dead.

As with many musical movements, the most accomplished, original and innovative players have the ability to transcend the genre they have (often reluctantly) been associated with. This is clearly the case with Blur, Suede and the Manic Street Preachers. Whilst they were quickly tagged by a Britpop-hungry media at the time, their music since the mid-90s has shown that they are creatively complex and artistically progressive. Blur's eponymous fifth album was a dramatic shift in direction with its hardcore-influenced, abrasive guitars and thunderous rhythmn section (best shown with the classic 'Song 2') winning major acclaim. Suede negotiated the loss of their guitarist and returned with the quite brilliant, chart-topping long player *Coming Up*, which was crammed with both classic singles and deeper, more pensive album tracks. The Manic Street Preachers similarly suffered the loss of a member (the tragic disappearance of Richey Edwards) but have since released two superb albums, most recently with their universally revered *This Is My Truth Tell Me Yours*.

On December 31st, 1994, Max Griggs received a CBE from Her Majesty The Queen for services to the footwear industry.

James Dean Bradfield of Manic Street Preachers

The video for Blur's 'The Universal' was based loosely around the iconography of Clockwork Orange.

"It will take its place in footwear sales on its merits. The prospects of export business are believed to be good."

Extract from Shoe & Leather News

Since the 1950s, British youth culture has proved to be one of the country's most consistent and popular exports. Although the Teddy Boy remained an essentially English peculiarity, since then generations of subcultural styles and music have crossed the globe, inevitably mutating in the process into a new hybrid - a cyclical and constant shredding and recycling of ideas. This international appeal has meant that DM's are perhaps Britain's most significant contribution to global anti-fashion and counter-culture in the last forty years. More importantly, the boot's iconic status has been created by the marketplace, not sold to it. What makes this more remarkable is the fact that until the '80s there were only a handful of styles.

Before the '80s, however, the boots limited export availability meant that DM's could only trickle abroad. That all changed in 1988. This year saw several notable events - George Bush followed two term Ronald Reagan into the Whitehouse, and (perhaps no coincidence) prozac was launched. It was also an important date for Dr. Martens - not because any new style was launched, nor because a new subculture latched on to the boot, but simply because of a supposedly mundane administrative happening: Airwair Export was created.

In America, the boot's restricted availability meant that prior to 1991, DM's were very difficult to find, although in some senses this gave some added kudos to the brand. The influx began in California, before spreading through word of mouth and amongst various subcultures to other cities. By 1993, the boot was grabbing headlines across the States for trouncing the trainer market that had been dominant for so long. Surfers, skateboarders, punks, grunge kids, metalheads and industrial fans were just a few of the subcultures who picked up on Dr. Martens.

Like in Britain, the boot has had its darker moments, mainly with the associations with neo-fascism. Some schools banned Docs from uniform lists because of what were seen as unsavoury connotations - one school in Grapevine, Texas suffered a pupil walk-out in protest after the decision to outlaw the boot. Generally, however, Doc Martens have proved very popular in the States, and provide a rare beacon of UK culture in America, after fifty years of post-war Americanisation of Great Britain.

In the Far East, the boot found a niche that blossomed quickly into a major phenomenon. Nearby China had for a long time suppressed the rise of rock music - indeed, the authorities once denounced rock 'n' roll as 'pornographic' and consequently banned it - a pamphlet was issued that was titled 'How to Recognise Pornographic Music' and even listed jazz. However, such oppression could not stop the growing interest and the impact of Western culture and music has created its own indigenous subculture. More recently, the reluctant party line was changed and limited scope was made for the modern music, with an official statement saying in certain cases it could be seen as "healthy exercise for young and old.'

Across in Hong Kong, matters were somewhat more liberal. Docs had filtered through in tiny quantities before 1990, but once the export gates were fully open, the country's thirst for British culture meant that the boots were a massive hit. Early 1994 saw a phase of bell bottoms worn with 1460s - elsewhere the 20 hole boots have proved very popular. Demand has become so great in certain areas that a thriving second-hand market has developed, with a few rare styles selling for more than brand new boots. Similar cult status has been afforded the boots in Japan, where the English culture and their own unique styles have seen the boot used in a myriad of ways.

Like America, Australasia's affair with Doc Martens was boosted with the arrival of grunge. In Germany, the boot's original homeland, some 100,000 pairs had been sold back by 1993. Empty container lorries from the Eastern Bloc and Russia have been known to pull up outside the Wollaston factory asking for hundreds of pairs to take back home. Even in France, which has traditionally been somewhat averse to British culture, the boot has found its own corner of the market. It is now a truly global icon.

Some Docs have been exported illegally with drugs stashed in the cavities in the sole, which is split open, filled with the illicit goods and then sealed with a hot-knife. Even some official export shipments of Dr. Martens have been stopped at Customs to check for this.

Rancid

Rancid are one of America's most compelling new bands. Mixing 2 Tone ska with Clash-influenced punk, covering Oi! band The Blitz and working with members of The Specials, they are indeed a strange mix. Their eponymous debut album started a run of independently released albums that put the fire back into a rapidly ailing *MTV* American rock circuit. Their second album was recorded and mixed in just four days. The third long player ...*And Out Come The Wolves* sold over half a million copies, and featured more of the lightning fast brevity, snarling lyrics and razor-sharp guitars that made their live shows such a riot. With their 1998 album *Life Won't Wait*, Rancid found themselves to be one of the biggest alternative bands on the planet.

When they were offered $1.5 million to sign to Epic Records, they declined, instead choosing to remain with their independent record company Epitaph, because "we're friends with just about everybody on the label."

Rob Zombie

Reverend Horton Heat

Slayer

On the
tour bus
with
Anthrax

Keith

Maxim

Leeroy

Liam

Prodigy

One American phenomenon of the late '90s that can be directly traced back to the exact kind of British heritage that Docs have been so heavily immersed in, is the ska revival led by bands like No Doubt and the Mighty Mighty Bosstones. This scene was itself preceded by a more underground wave of bands such as Weaker Youth Ensemble, the Allstonians, Bim Skala Bim, the Voodoo Glow Skulls and The Toasters. This last band once called themselves Not Bob Marley and have been instrumental to the popularity of ska music in the US. Known by observers as 'the third wave of ska', this movement started evolving into a commercial behemoth in 1996, when alongside No Doubt and the Mighty Mighty Bosstones came bands like Smash Mouth, Goldfinger, and Reel Big Fish - these bands' multi-platinum success took ska-influenced music on to a commercially enormous scale. Purists aired grievances as to the viability of some of these bands' variants on the originals, but the very essence of subcultures and music is that each new generation takes from its own environment and makes something new of its own.

The huge success of bands like these provided a genuine alternative to the post-grunge rock bands that were filling *MTV*'s schedules. Most interesting of all is their eclectic mix of influences - not just ska but also metal, hardcore, hip hop, and even classical music has been used to great effect by this new wave of musicians. Whilst the 2 Tone phenomenon provided a glimpse of British youth at the turn of the '80s, then this third wave showed just how multicultural and varied the American youth of today have become.

Not surprisingly, when bands draw on such disparate ideas, styles and music, Docs are bound to crop up. The influence of Madness, Bad Manners, British punk bands, Mods and even skinhead music was prevalent and rapidly assimilated by this new wave of culture-hungry kids. Hence, sometimes two or even three decades after original British cults found Docs on their feet, the boots and shoes were being pulled on by Americans a generation younger.

"This third wave showed just how multicultural and varied the American youth of today was."

The Toasters

Arguably the highest profile and most successful of all these bands is the chart topping No Doubt. Hailing from California, they played for over seven years before their superb album, *Tragic Kingdom,* went global, spearheaded by the international hit single 'Don't Speak' and boosted by the follow-up smashes 'Just a Girl' and 'Spiderwebs'. The band's beautiful lead singer, Gwen Stefani, was wearing a pair of red DM's on the album's cover and has since accumulated a huge collection of Docs, many of which have been custom made.

Gwen Stefani's brother dropped out of the band to become a cartoonist for The Simpsons.

The late '70s second wave of British ska enjoyed only limited commercial success in America, although bands like Her Majesties Secret Service did bring the 2 Tone sound to the country in the early '80s.

Also in the '90s: It took radio over 40 years to get a global audience of 50 million; it took television 15 years to do the same. The Internet achieved that in less than 36 months.

No Doubt

"Living in a **college** town all my life like I do, the **subways**, streets and crowded **nightclubs** are full now with Dr. Martens, but I remember a **time** when it was just me and a **handful** of friends that wore them."

Dicky Barrett

Boston's Mighty Mighty Bosstones are in many ways the perfect example of what can happen when various subcultures collide together in one frenetic, multi-faceted amalgam. Formed in 1985 (originally as just the Bosstones), the band had been pioneering their blend of musical genres for years before the mainstream picked up on their sound and labelled them 'third wave ska'. In fact, the Bosstones are much more than that, with lead singer Dicky Barrett himself describing their sound as "a punk/ska hybrid."

They are a racially mixed and musically diverse outfit, fusing backgrounds in acts such as ska band the Cheapskates and the seminal hardcore group Gang Green, whilst drawing on the past glories of bands such as the Specials and the Clash. The whole previous four decades of subculture seem to find a place in the multitude of elements of this band.

Until recently, much of their business was done on a gentlemen's handshake, including booking national tours independently. The cumulative effect of this, and their almost rabid following, was the global smash single, 'The Impression That I Get', and the corresponding album *Let's Face It*. These two records marked a commerical high point for the Bosstones, but behind this success lay nearly a decade of musical experimentation.

To complement the music, the band support a variety of causes, including Anti-Racist Action, the National Clinic Access Project and several battered women shelters. Nate Albert admitted to being delighted when *The New York Times* dubbed the band "ska punk with a social consience."

Mighty Mighty Bosstones

Red Hot Chili Peppers

give it away

Doc Facts

10,000 fake Docs have been seized by AirWair and re-distributed to homeless and war charities; An old wives tale says if you collect shoes then you are a frustrated traveller — the average American woman has 30 pairs; At the infamous 'Rave at the Nave', where techno music was played to amassed converts, most followers wore Docs; Griggs have supported education programmes, the Prince's Youth Business Trust, Shelter, Childline, the National Youth Theatre and Wollaston School; Alexei Sayle sings about the merits of Doc Martens on his album *Cak*; Matthew Gregory has the world's biggest feet: size 29.5. He weighs 330 pounds, stands 7' 6"...and wears DM's; Griggs is still a private family business, not a public company; The prototypes for the Open AirWair range were made for a Polaris submarine crew; Each boot uses 2.5 square feet of leather and over 100 individual operations; The average person walks five times round the world or half way to the moon in their lifetime; You can now use the word 'Docs' in Scrabble, as it is officially recognised in The Oxford Dictionary; In the early '60s, 5000 pairs were made a week — now that figure is 200,000; In 1984, the UK's Football League kicked out a lucrative sponsorship deal because of the boot's bovver boy image; Vegetarian Dr. Martens are made from a material often used on yachts; Crack SAS troops wore them in the Falklands War; There have been over 3000 styles available; Doc Martens have their own tartan, called MacMarten Tartan; In 1990, readers of the *NME* voted Docs their 'Fashion Item of the Year'; AirWair use 42,000 kilometres of yellow stitching every year, and ten million laces — Each year they use 4.5 million square metres of leather — the equivalent of 650 football pitches; London Contemporary Dance Theatre, the Royal Shakespeare Company and the Toronto Contemporary Dance Company are just a few production companies who've used Dr.Martens; Dr. Martens are currently the No. 1 welted shoe manufacturer in the world.

Stephen Griggs

The current Chairman, Stephen Griggs, is the fifth generation of Griggs to run the company. He was born the year after the 1460 was launched and for the first eleven years of his life lived next door to the company headquarters. His old bedroom is now an AirWair office. He left school aged 16, and became a trainee accountant, before spending a year studying shoemaking at Wellingborough Technical College. He joined his father's company aged 21, and his first task lasted six months, sticking felt pads into the soles of the boots. He took over as group Chairman in 1993.

AfterWord

It is, indeed, a strange story. Dr. Martens have almost inadvertently attained a status and cultural significance that could never have been forseen back in April, 1960. Almost from the outset, DM's have won a diverse allegiance from an incredible array of subcultures. With each shift in youth fashion and thinking, new generations have moulded the shoe and recycled it for their own ends, each time injecting it with new subcultural potency which in turn has been mimicked by the next generation, heaping yet more heritage on its simple shape. As the millennium spins ever nearer, and modern media blurs subcultures into one another with frightening speed, Doc Martens still appear to hold their own.

The original 1460 is clearly a modern design classic. Internationally there are only a handful of designs that can boast similar status. Ray Bans, Levis, the VW Beetle, Zippo Lighters, Marlboro cigarettes, the black leather jacket. In Britain, the list is far smaller. The Mini motorcar. Fred Perrys. It is a select few. What once was a bulbous and plain workwear boot is now a good-looking subcultural essential. It has become the perfect integration of both form and fashion.

Dr. Martens are one of the oddest fashion trends of all time. They fit with boiler suits, combats, pinstripes, bondage trousers or flowery dresses. They will probably be around as long as people have feet. They have always annoyed your parents. They remain the first and only boot of its kind on the market. Like the subcultures that created them, they are scruffy, smart, sexy, macho, fashionable, fashionless, classy, classless, uniform, unique. They are Dr. Martens.

Acknowledgements and Bibliography

The following publications have provided invaluable research material: *Spirit of '69, A Skinhead Bible* by George Marshall, ST Publishing 1991, ISBN 1-898927-10-3; *England's Dreaming* by Jon Savage, Faber & Faber, 1991, ISBN 0-571-16791-8; *Our Times - The Illustrated History of the 20th Century*, Ed. Lorraine Glennon, Turner Publishing Inc., 1995, ISBN 1-878685-58-9; *British Cultural Identities*, Ed. Mike Storry & Peter Childs, Routledge, 1997, ISBN 0-415-13699-7; *The New Book of Rock Lists*, by Dave Marsh & James Bernard, Sidgwick & Jackson, 1994, ISBN 0-283-06181-2; *Jabberock* by Raymond Obstfeld & Patricia Fitzgerald, Canongate Books Ltd, 1997, ISBN 0-86241-757-0; *Scooter Boys* by Gareth Brown, Omnibus Press, 1996, ISBN 0-7119-6159-X; *Camden Girls* by Jane Owen, Penguin, 1997, ISBN 0-14-026424-8; *Slade* by George Tremlett, Futura Publications Ltd, 1975, ISBN 0-8600-7193-6; *You're Wondering Now - A History of The Specials* by Paul Williams, ST Publishing, 1995, ISBN 1-898927-25-1; *The Two Tone Story* by George Marshall, ST Publishing, 1990, ISBN 0-95184973-5; *Route 666 - On The Road To Nirvana* by Gina Arnold, St Martin's Press Inc., 1993, ISBN 0-330-32931-6; *Prodigy - The Fat of the Land* by Martin Roach & The Prodigy, Independent Music Press, 1997, ISBN 1-897783-12-4; *Street Style* by Ted Polhemus, Thames & Hudson, 1994, ISBN 0-500-27794-X; *The All Music Book of Hit Albums*, by Dave McAleer, Miller Freeman Books, 1995, ISBN 0-87930-393-X; *The All Music Book of Hit Singles*, by Dave McAleer, Miller Freeman Books, 1994, ISBN 0-87930-425-1; *The Soccer Tribe* by Desmond Morris, Jonathan Cape, 1981, ISBN 0-224-01935-X; *The NME Rock 'n' Roll Years*, Ed. John Tobler, Reed International Books Ltd, 1990, ISBN 0-600-57016-9; *Surfers, Soulies, Skinheads & Skaters*, by Amy De La Haye & Cathie Dingwall, Victoria & Albert Museum, 1996, ISBN 1-85177-175-1; *Mods!* by Richard Barnes, Plexus, 1979, ISBN 0-85965-173-8; *Subculture - The Meaning of Style* by Dick Hebdige, Routledge, 1979, ISBN 0-415-03949-5; *The Alternative Music Almanac*, by Alan Cross, Collector's Guide Publishing Inc., 1995, ISBN 1-896522-14-9; *Our Culture*, by Fred Skarface; *Tribes of England* by Fred Skarface; *Total Madness* by George Marshall, ST Publishing, 1993, ISBN 0-9518497-4-3; *Rolling Stone - Images of Rock & Roll*, Little, Brown, 1995, ISBN 1-85227-518-9; *Haircults* by Dylan Jones, Thames & Hudson, 1990, ISBN 0-500-275688; *The Gothic Rock Black Book*, by Mick Mercer, Omnibus Press, 1988, ISBN 0-7119-1546-6; *Punk! An A-Z*, by Barry Lazell, Hamlyn, 1995, ISBN 0-600-58635-9; *Images of Punk*, by Denis O' Regan, Castle Communications Plc., 1996, ISBN 1-86074-162-2; *Alt.Culture - An A-Z of the 90s*, by Steven Daly and Nathaniel Wice, Fourth Estate Ltd., 1995, ISBN 1-85702-378-1; *Punk Diary 1970-1979*, by George Gimarc, Vintage, 1994, ISBN 0-09-952211-X; *Skinhead*, Nick Knight, Omnibus Press, 1982, ISBN 0-7119-0052-3; *Skins* by Gavin Watson, ST Publishing, 1994, ISBN 1-898927-05-7; *Buzzcocks - The Complete History*, by Tony McGartland, Independent Music Press, 1995, ISBN 1-897783-05-1; *The Eight Legged Atomic Dustbin Will Eat Itself*, by Martin Roach, Independent Music Press, 1992, ISBN 1-897783-00-0; *A Time To Travel*, by Fiona Earle, Alan Dearling, Helen Whittle, Roddy Glasse and Gubby, Enabler Publications, 1994, ISBN 0-9523316-08; *Markenkult*, Ed. Matthias Horx, Peter Wippermann, Trendburo, 1995; *Shoes, Fashion and Fantasy* by Colin McDowell, Thames & Hudson, 1989; *Heavenly Soles - Extraordinary 20th Century Shoes* by Mary Trasko, Abbeville Press, USA, ISBN 1-55859-324-1, 1992; *Shoes - A Celebration of Pumps, Sandals, Slippers and More*, by Linda O'Keefe, Workman Publishing New York 1996 ISBN 0-7611-0114-4; *A Century of Shoes - Icons of Style in the 20th Century*, by Angela Pattison and Nigel Cawthorne, Page One Pub. Pte. Ltd, 1997, ISBN 981-00-9216-4

Homeless Statistics: Taken from *Young People and Homelessness*, a pamphlet provided by Shelter. Statistics apply to the UK and are taken (in order) from Homeless People, DOE, HMSO, 1993 by I. Anderson, P. Kemp and D. Quilgars; *The New Picture of Youth Homelessness*, Centrepoint, 1996; St. Mungo's Press Release, May 1996. Kind thanks to Shelter for this literature and their assistance.

Miscellaneous Articles: A superb article and interview with Dr Klaus Maertens in *The Daily Mail* by Cindi Payne, 20/2/85 ; Article in *The Scotsman* by Thea Jourdan, 6/4/96 ; Article in *The Shoe & Leather News* by Judith Gaskell, 4/1/85 ; Looking Good 3/88; 'A Brief Shoe History' from *The Financial Times* by James Ferguson, 31/10/87; 'Objects of Desire' in *Weiner Magazine* by Ulla Jacobs, 11/92; Article in *The Independent* by Roger Tredre, 12/9/92; 'Just What the Doctor Ordered' in *Commerce* Magazine by Tony Boullemier, 2/94; Article on Dr. Martens in Aer Lingus' In-Flight magazine by Mary Dowey, 1993; Article in *City Limits* by Dave Hill, 19-25/10/84; Article in *Ragtrader* by Kate Lyons, 15/2/94; Article in *Sunday Life* by Neil Mulholland, 20/6/93; 'Fifty Years of Fashions, Fads and Cults' in *The Daily Mail* by Tony Thorne, 17/3/93; Article in *Appointment* Magazine, 2/97; 'The Good Life - Report From Boot Camp', by Dan Ackerman, unknown publication; 'Eyewitness' - Article on the first Glastonbury Festival in *Q* by Johnny Black, 7/96; 'The Death of Tribes' feature in *Q*, by Andrew Smith, 11/97; Article on Dr. Martens in *The Face* by Neil Spencer, 4/86; Sleeve liner notes for *The Who - Who's Better, Who's Best* by Richard Barnes.

Web Credits:
Punk: http://www.film.queensu.ca/Chamberlain4.html by Bryn Chamberlain; *Footwear History:* from http://www.fenice.com/footware_history. html; *Festivals:* http:// www.visi.com/~astanley/rad/ by Adam Stanley; *Skinheads:* http://www.zebra.net/~mdjones/page_standup_skinhead.html;

The following magazines have also proved invaluable: NME, Melody Maker, Record Collector, Q, Vox, Select, Rolling Stone, Oz Magazine, The Times, The Daily Mail, The Daily Express, The Face, Loaded, What's Up Doc, Footwear, Alternative Press. Also The Airwair Archive; *The Shoe & Leather News*; The Northampton Shoe Museum Archive.

Every effort has been made to fully and correctly credit and source all material used in this book. The publishers would be grateful if any errors were brought to their attention.

Photo Credits in order of appearance and clockwise on page:
Pg 2: Bgrd: Pete Anderson; 3: Nils Jorgensen/Rex Features; 4 & 5: R. Griggs Archive; 6 & 7: Gavin Watson; 8: Beddall/The Times/Rex; Today/Rex; Dennis Hutchinson/Rex; 9: Paul Slattery; 10: P. P. Harnett/Rex; 11: James Ferguson; 12 & 13: Gavin Watson; 14: P. P. Harnett/Rex; SIPA/Rex; Bgrd: Gavin Watson; 15: Gavin Watson; 16: Gavin Watson; 17: Gavin Watson; Richard Allen book cover courtesy of ST Publishing; 19: Pennie Smith; 20: R. Griggs Archive; 21: Centre pic: Paul Brown/Rex; Outside pics: Gareth Brown; 22: Gavin Watson; 24: From 'Skinhead Bible' by ST Publishing; 25: Jill Furmanovsky/JFA; 27: Brian Moody/Rex; 28: Roger Bamber/Rex; 29: Courtesy of Ian Dury; 31: Denis O' Regan; 32: Nick Rogers/Rex; 33: Nils Jorgensen/Rex; 34: Denis O' Regan; Bgrd: Peter Stuart/Rex; Ray Steveson/Rex; 35: Pennie Smith; Keith Morris; 36: Brendan Beirne/Rex; Text by Pete Shelley; 37: Gavin Watson; 38: Zbysiu Rodak/S.I.N; 40: David Levenson/Rex; 41: Gavin Watson; 43: Jill Furmanovsky/JFA; 44: Philip Green/All Action; 45 & 46: Flyers and poster taken from 'The Two Tone Story by ST Publishing; 47: Scarlet Page; 48 & 49: Kevin Cummins/Retna; 50: Ian Tilton/S.I.N; 51: Sean Brady; Madness CD sleeve appears courtesy of Virgin Records: Photography by Alexandra Burke; Design by Mark Bedford, Vicky Fullick and Steven Davis; 52: Sheila Rock/Retna; 53: Text by Lee Thompson; 54: Victor Boullet; 56: The Meteors; 57: Text by Martin Millar; Nils Jorgensen/Rex; Martin Hampton; Martin Hampton; Russ Hancox; Martin Hampton; 58: Iain McKell/Retna; 59: Neil Matthews/Retna; 60: Jean Tran; 61: Sean Brady; Andrew Catlin/S.I.N; Adrian Boot; 62: Mark Taylor; 63: Steven Morrissey/Linda Sterling; 64: Ed Sirrs/Retna; 65: Martyn Goodacre; Kevin Westerberg/Chrysalis Records; 66: Jill Furmanovsky/JFA; 67: Jill Furmanovsky/JFA; Martyn Goodacre; 68: Courtesy of Exclusive Copyright owners, Island Records; 69: Neil Mackenzie Matthews; 70: Peter Brooker/Rex; Julian Makey/Rex; Scarlet Page; 71: Ken McKay/Rex; Tony Larkin/Rex; Dave Hogan/Rex; 72 & 73: Pete Anderson; 74: Nils Jorgensen/Rex; Brian Rasic/Rex; Justin Thomas/All Action; Nils Jorgensen/Rex; Lesley Smith/Rex; 75: Bgrd: Pete Anderson; Andy Soloman/Rex; 77: Martyn Goodacre; 78: Bgrd: Rex; Martyn Goodacre; 79: Melanie Cox; Hayley Madden/S.I.N; Yan Morvan/Rex; 80: Duncan Phillips/Rex; 81: Brendan Beirne/Rex; Nick Bailey/Rex; Andrew Dunsmore/Rex; 82: Nick Bailey/Rex; Richard Gardner/Rex; Brookes/The Times/Rex; SIPA/Rex; 83: Greg Williams/Rex; 84: Bgrd: Martyn Goodacre; 85: Today/Rex; Peter Brooker/Rex; Jeremy Sutton-Hibbert/Rex; 86: Martyn Goodacre; 87: David Corio/S.I.N; 89: John Shard; 91: Steve Gullick; 93: Anton Corbijn; 95: Paul Stanley/S.I.N; 96: Colin Bell/EMI Records; 97: Chris Floyd/All Action; 99: SIPA/Rex; 100: B. J. Papas; 101: Brian Rasic/Rex; Michael Levine; Chris McCann; Kirsten Mulderig; 102 & 103: Steve Gullick; 104: Dale Rio; 105: Pat Pope/Rex; 106 & 107: Danny Clinch; 108: From the Red Hoto Chili Peppers' video 'Give It Away' used courtesy of Warner Bros. Records. Inc.; 110: Gavin Watson; The Shakespeare Centre: Joe Cocks Theatre Collection; 111: Gavin Watson; 112: Gavin Watson.

Every effort has been made to trace the copyright holders of the photographs in this book, but one or two were unreachable. The publisher would be grateful if the photographers concerned would contact AirWair Limited.

The Quadrophenia logo appears by kind permission of Trinifold Management Ltd/The Who.
Still from the Red Hot Chili Peppers' video 'Give It Away' appears by courtesy of Warner Bros. Records Inc.
New Boots and Panties album sleeve appears by kind permission of Ian Dury.
Madness - The Business CD sleeve appears courtesy of Virgin Records.

Dr. Martens on the Web: www.drmartens.com

The author would like to thank: Angus Batey, Bones, Gareth Brown, Chris Burton, Kevin Caan, Philip Conway, Cheryl Farmer, Philip Gambrill, Geroge Goble, Steve Gullick, Andrew King, Steve Lamacq, Steve Lake, Marianne Lassen, Andy Linihan, George Marshall, Glenn Marx, Martin Millar, Jane Owen, Mark Radcliffe, Marc Riley, Paolo Scaramuzza, Mike Shea, Gavin Watson, Paul Wolf and all at Dr. Martens. Dedicated to Kaye Roach . Special thanks to Tony and Diane Roach, Stu and Deb, Joe, Simon and Tracey Dunn, Jessica, Alma Hazlewood, Nina and Stewart Potter, Vegan, Stuart Coles, Steve Fellows, the Welches, Rebecca Hill. Up the Villa!

Gary Pettet would like to thank: Sylvia Morris and the Royal Shakespeare Company, Jonathan Kessler, Martin Gore, Steve Boakes, LP, Pompey Mark, Adrian Boss, Emma, Nigel Hasler, Chrissy Yiannou, Lol Pryor, Sonia, Toast, Mark Brennan, Anton Brookes and Badmoon, Ginni Keith, Roland and Russell, Kirsten at Concrete, Neve and Kate at CMO, Karen Johnson, Jody, Michelle Fenech, Stuart Osborne, Russ Hancox, Trish Simonon, Charlie Charlton and Interceptor, Sarah Miller, Rik Rogers, Steve Blackwell, Peter Rudge, Dave Tomberlin at Interscope, Sally McKewon at Principle, Vicki Wickham, Debbie, Sherry, Sarah Yeoman, Francesca Hicks, Barbara and Richard Bishop at 3AM, Q Prime, Doug at Hydrogen Jukebox, Bruce Duff, Tiny Fennimore, Andy Swallow and Phil at Labello, Andy Cowan-Martin, Jenny Stanley Clark, Joe Cashman, Doug James at Gold Mountain, Liz at Hall Or Nothing, Sill Wilcox, Helena Coram at Warners, Emma Duyts at Warners, Trevor Long, Mark Young, Martin 'Chunky' Hampton, Scott Weiss and Charles at Electric, Lisa Barker, Mick Gerrie, Howard at Raucous, Emma Banks, Charlie Myatt, Dean Wengrow, Digger Barnes, Gerrard Myers, Sue at Mute Press, Mitch Okmin, Francis Priest, Bill Curbishley, Daryl Bamonte, Micky Fitz, Paul Woolf, Andy Franks, Norman Watt Roy, Mick Gallagher, Raff Edmonds, Charlie Inskip, Gary Crowley, Kevin Sampson, Paul Oremland, Paul Boswell, Nichola Joss, Mick B and Errol, Mitch Okmin, Francis Priest, Tracy at SFA, Kim Holt, Barbara Dowling, Mike Hinc, Steve Payne, Mo Green and Annie, Boz Boorer, Debbie Diamond, Imogen Hollingsworth, Ami Bennet, Simon Mills, Louise Mayne, Peter Young, The Levellers, Madeleine, Dave Chumbly, Paul Franklyn, Pellicis in Bethnal Green.
Thank you to my beautiful wife Mitra, Mum, Dad and Jan. Play up Pompey!

Many thanks to the following for their involvement: John Peel, Billy Bragg, Tony Benn MP, Pete Townshend, Noddy Holder, Ian Dury, Paul Simonon, Jean Jacques Burnel and The Stranglers, Catwoman, Rat Scabies and The Damned, Pete Shelley, Joe Strummer, Jerry Dammers, Terry Hall, Buster Bloodvessel, Madness, Lee Thompson, Sioxsie Sioux, Budgie, The Creatures, The Meteors, King Kurt, Smeg, Guana Batz, Pip Hancox, Martin Millar, Paul King, Simon Gallup, Robert Smith, The Cure, Alan Wilder, Shane McGowan, Sean McCluskey, Jo Boxers, Morrissey, Boz, Rat, Carter USM, Blessed Ethel, Polly Harvey, Sinéad O' Connor, Mik Scarlet, Peter Stringfellow, Mark Chadwick, Rev Hammer, The Levellers, Kate Adie, Tad, Foo Fighters, Henry Rollins, Depeche Mode, Martin Gore, Anton Corbijn, Manic Street Preachers, James Dean Bradfield, Blur, Suede, Rancid, Rob Zombie, Slayer, Reverend Horton Heat, Anthrax, Liam Howlett, Maxim, Leeroy Thornhill, Keith Flint, The Toasters, No Doubt, Mighty Mighty Bosstones, Red Hot Chili Peppers.

Thanks to Stephen Griggs and Frank Duffy for their assistance in the making of this book.